Managing a Company in an Activist World

The Leadership Challenge of Corporate Citizenship

EDMUND M. BURKE

Westport, Connecticut
London

Library of Congress Cataloging-in-Publication Data

Burke, Edmund M.
   Managing a company in an activist world : the leadership challenge of corporate
citizenship / Edmund M. Burke.
      p. cm.
   Includes bibliographical references and indexes.
   ISBN 0–275–98390–0 (alk. paper)
      1. Social responsibility of business.   2. Industrial management—Social
aspects.   3. Corporations—Public relations.   I. Title.
   HD60.B858   2005
   658.4′08—dc22   2004022588

British Library Cataloguing in Publication Data is available.

Library of Congress Catalog Card Number: 2004022588
ISBN: 0–275–98390–0

First published in 2005

Praeger Publishers, 88 Post Road West, Westport, CT 06881
An imprint of Greenwood Publishing Group, Inc.
www.praeger.com

Printed in the United States of America

The paper used in this book complies with the
Permanent Paper Standard issued by the National
Information Standards Organization (Z39.48–1984).

10 9 8 7 6 5 4 3 2 1

To Lee
my inspiration

Note

Fifty percent of the author's proceeds from this book will be donated to The Center for Corporate Citizenship at Boston College

Contents

Preface   ix

Acknowledgments   xiii

1   With Apologies to James Carville . . .   1
    "It's the Behavior, Stupid"

2   The Case for Change   11

3   The Faces of Activism   29

4   Step One: You Start with a Vision—A Social Vision   45

5   Step Two: Abandon the Command and Control Style   57
    of Managing External Affairs

6   Step Three: Use the CACDIC Strategy   69

7   Step Four: Who Are Our External Stakeholders   79
    and What Do They Value?

8   Step Five: What Are the Characteristics of Our   91
    Relationships?

9   Preparing Managers for the New New Thing   101

10   The Stakeholder Relations Plan   121

11   The Site Community Strategy: A Responsibility of   123
    the Facility Manager

12 The Site Community Strategy, Continued   139

13 The Societal Strategy—The CEO's Responsibility   155

Notes   173

Name Index   183

Subject Index   189

Preface

Corporate citizenship has become the "new new thing." The old arguments that the business of business is business and that corporations have no obligation or even the right to become involved in the community are no longer made.

Even William Safire, the conservative columnist for the *New York Times* who labeled corporate responsibility "the new socialism," now acknowledges that "good community relations help attract the best managers and innovators to a company."[1]

Yet, there is no universal agreement among mangers on why corporate citizenship is necessary. Doing good—one more burdensome task—has for one group of managers become a necessity because the consequences can be costly. As McKinsey & Co. tells its clients, "Apparent irresponsibility can carry a high price,"[2] The new new thing is something we have to do. (Incidentally, the "won't do" manager is not worth mentioning. It is a vanishing breed.)

For another group of managers, the new new thing is an opportunity—the doing well by doing good crowd. Dozens of studies claim that the public prefers to buy products from companies that are socially responsible. Indeed, the guru of competitiveness, Harvard Business School professor Michael Porter, is consulting with companies, helping them to use their community involvement practices to obtain a competitive advantage.[3] Doing good, in other words, makes business sense, and it is obviously something we ought to do.

And then there is a third group of managers, called social visionaries by the Dean of the Yale School of Management, Jeffrey Garten, who claim that corporate citizenship is a value to be sought regardless of its pragmatic advantages. It is the right thing to do. It is something "we want to do."

Regardless of motives, the three types of managers—the have to do's, the ought to do's, and the want to do's—all ask the same questions. What do I need to know as a manager—and please don't complicate the simple and make my job more time consuming than it already is—to make corporate citizenship a success in my company? In other words: How do I manage it?

The purpose of this book is to answer that question. It is written for the general manager. While community relations managers, philanthropy foundation executives, ethics officers, and environmental vice presidents, for example, should find this book valuable and interesting, the audience is plant and facility managers, senior executives, presidents and chief executive officers. It is they, after all, who are ultimately held accountable for the success or failure of a business enterprise.

In fact, it is the site or facility manager who is becoming increasingly responsible for the reputation and image of the company in its various communities. The community relations manager is fast becoming a facilitator for the site manager, aiding in planning, developing training, organizing meetings in the community for site and general managers, and providing information and data to design and evaluate strategies.

The responsibility for the design and operation of the global or societal strategy falls to the CEO. Assisted by a variety of specialists and senior officers, the CEO is held accountable for the success of the global citizenship strategy.

Managing the new new thing is not difficult or complicated. It does require changes in managers' behavior and attitudes. Managers have to be willing to understand and respond to changing expectations for corporate performance. It requires, too, a plan. The casual off-the-cuff, shoot-from-the-hip approach to developing what I call trust relationships with external stakeholders no longer works. It requires thought and conscientiousness, just as much thought and conscientiousness as goes into managing employees.

Thankfully, over the past dozen years, a growing body of knowledge has emerged that makes managing corporate citizenship doable. Much of it is based on the experience of companies that were thrust into the fray of community activism in the 1980s and 1990s. And still more is based on the work of scholars and researchers associated with business schools and nongovernmental organizations.

One such organization is The Center for Corporate Citizenship at Boston College, an organization that I founded in 1985. I rely heavily on the staff work of The Center and my work with companies associated with The Center for the material presented in this book. I use freely and with acknowledgment the formal research and studies published by The Center. In fact, one of The Center's most useful reports is an annual survey of over 400 community relations and foundation executives that is conducted during the seminars and institutes run by The Center. Because the surveys are completed while attending a program, the response rate is commonly over 95 percent. Arguably, no other report describing and analyzing the continuing changes companies are making to adapt to the new demands and expectations of communities is as reliable and as valid.

I also rely on my research and experience in politics and community planning. I served on the Domestic Policy staff of the White House under President Jimmy Carter, where I was responsible for promoting strategic planning among the federal agencies. I planned and managed the first White House Conference on Strategic Planning in 1979.

I was engaged in the professional practice of community planning, taught and conducted research in community planning for twenty-five years, and served as the dean of Boston College's Graduate School of Social Work. I cite this experience deliberately, because community analysis and planning have become an integral part of a company's citizenship practices. Success in today's new society requires a company to advocate for a point of view, much like that of a community planning and social policy organization.

To enable that point of view to be considered fairly and honestly, managers have to understand how a community makes decisions. They have to know who gets involved in the process of community decision making. They need also to be sensitive to the unique culture and values of the communities and societies in which they operate. Community planning practice and experience, consequently, can provide a critical background to any company's corporate citizenship strategies.

I cite this experience and background to help the reader understand the basis for the points I am making in this book.

Acknowledgments

I want to thank a great many people who contributed to the work of writing this book. Some did it knowingly by making comments, suggestions, and opening new ideas and courses of inquiry. They include Greg Anderegg, SC Johnson Wax; Charles Borgognoni, formerly of Bristol-Myers Squibb; Sheila Carruthers, formerly of Canadian Pacific; Brian Cosgrove, SIAC; Ann Cramer, IBM; Suzanne Hoffmon Esber, Fluor Corporation; Lewis Karabatsos, H-P, Michael Kehoe, Ameritech; Virginia McEnerney, Time Warner; Jane Newlands, BC Hydro; Mary O'Malley, Prudential; Ann Pomykal, Texas Instruments; Brad Simmons, Ford Motor Company; David Thomas, Sprint; Richard Trabert, formerly with Merck and Co.; Laura Tew, Arch Chemicals; and Noel Wheeler, formerly with Shell Chemical.

Those who unknowingly helped me were participants in the executive education seminars I conducted for The Center. We were all involved in uncovering and explaining the new directions of their companies efforts to implement the values and practices of the new corporate citizenship. They were part of a work in progress, and I deeply appreciate their assistance.

There are also staff members of The Center for Corporate Citizenship at Boston College who gave me ideas, reviewed what I had written, and went out of their way to find research material and sources of information. They include Bradley Googins, executive director of The Center, along with David Abdow, Kathleen Bannan, Eileen Blinstrub, Ronald Brown, Billy Brittingham, Paula Grealish, Kim Heck, Pauline Lonergan, Patty McLaughlin, Colleen Olphert, Steve Rochlin, Sapna Shah, Susan Thomas, Kathleen Witter, and Kristen Zecchi.

CHAPTER 1

With Apologies to James Carville . . . "It's the Behavior, Stupid"

The three essential tasks of management: (1) to establish the specific purpose and mission of the organization, (2) to make work productive and the worker efficient, (3) to manage the social impacts and social responsibilities of the company.
                                                                    —Peter Drucker

Corporate contributions to charities have more than doubled since 1990. CEOs are setting up billion dollar foundations to support their social causes. Employee volunteer programs can be found in almost all corporations. Business partnerships with community agencies and public schools are expanding. And corporations are publicizing their "good works" in newspapers, magazines, and annual reports. Never in history have corporations been more involved in social and community causes and never have they paid more attention to their public image as they do today.

Yet the hostility to business everywhere has never been higher. Protests, demonstrations, and boycotts against companies are increasing, wreaking havoc on corporate planning and strategy development.

Example: A local historical society stops The Walt Disney Company from opening a theme park in northern Virginia, a long-sought dream of the company's CEO, Michael Eisner.

Example: A single mother forces the Iroquois Pipe Line to rebuild a pipe line that results in a fine of $22 million and the criminal conviction of the CEO for his actions in violating the Clean Water Act.

Example: A retired couple in Naples, Florida, organizes residents to force U.S. Home Corporation, one of the nation's largest home builders, to withdraw its zoning request to build forty-five residential units on land the company owns.

Example: Residents of Inglewood, California, vote to deny Wal-Mart permission to build a superstore.

Example: AIDS activists shut down the New York Stock Exchange.

Example: Advocates for the disabled halt access to Greyhound bus terminals in New York.

Example: Fleet Financial Group is forced by neighborhood activists in Boston to contribute $20 million for inner-city loans because of lending violations.

Activist opposition is also spreading beyond the traditional community concerns to a variety of societal issues.

Example: Human rights organizations force the apparel industry, including Liz Claiborne, Nike, Reebok, Tommy Hilfiger, and Gap, to adopt an anti-sweatshop code of conduct in developing nations monitored for compliance by independent accounting firms.

Example: Environmental groups are stopping Monsanto from producing and marketing bio-engineered crop seed in Europe and Africa.

Example: A group of nuns halt Baxter International, one of the largest manufacturers of healthcare products, from using plastic in the manufacture of their intravenous tubes and bags.

Example: Local fishermen in Punta Abreojos, Mexico, stop Mitsubishi Corporation's plans to build a salt plant.

Example: Greenpeace organizes protests in the United Kingdom and Germany to successfully prevent Shell U.K. from disposing of a used oil rig in the North Atlantic.

Example: A small group of Indonesian farmers insist that ExxonMobil negotiate with them before it is allowed to begin oil exploration.

Example: The European Commission wants companies to adopt a uniform code of citizenship practices.

Example: Computer companies are pressured to solve the problem of the digital divide and make products available at prices that the poor in developing nations can afford.

Example: Students force universities to include a code of social responsibility conduct for manufacturers selling products in college bookstores.

Example: Pepsi Cola, in response to threats of a worldwide boycott of its products, withdraws from marketing its products in dictatorial Myanmar.

Example: The Association of British Insurers is requiring member companies to disclose how social, environmental, and ethical risks are being handled.

Example: Activists succeed in forcing the General Electric Company to dredge forty miles of the Hudson River at a cost estimated to exceed half a billion dollars.

Example: Threatened by a boycott, Toyota agrees to spend $8 billion to diversify its workforce.

Example: Hundreds of women stage a takeover of a ChevronTexaco terminal in Nigeria, demanding that the company build schools, roads, and hospitals and provide electricity and water for their communities. News of the demonstration fosters protests across Africa against other companies, including Royal Dutch Shell.

Now the protests are turning violent. When Shell U.K. announced it was planning to dispose of an oil rig, three gas stations were firebombed in Germany and over fifty were strafed with bullets. Gas wells have been blown up in Canada. A farmer in France was hailed as a hero after he ransacked a McDonald's restaurant. Chemists working for pharmaceutical companies have been sent threatening letters. Houses and condominiums in Long Island, New York, and Vail, Colorado, have been burned down by environmentalists. And the violence at the World Trade Organization (WTO) meeting that began in Seattle in November 1999 has become a commonplace event at meetings of world economic and trade organizations. One protestor was killed by the Italian police in Genoa, Italy, in August 2001.

Although there was hope that the events of 9/11 would reduce the violence, they have not. Fringe environmental and animal rights groups announced they would continue with violent protests. Indeed, shortly after 9/11, there was a firebombing at a federal horse corral, an arson fire at a primate research center, and break-ins to release animals at research farms. Groups such as the Animal Liberation Front and the Earth Liberation Front claim responsibility.[1] Anti-globalization is a twenty-year-old movement that has the support of private and corporate foundations, church groups, organized labor, and celebrities, and it is unlikely to go away.

There is, as well, a growing sentiment that supports the anger, if not the violence, of the protestors. In a cover story on a Harris poll conducted in August 2000, *BusinessWeek* magazine reported that 72 percent of Americans believed corporations have too much power over too many aspects of their lives. The respondents revealed a great deal of underlying anger directed at corporations for what they believed was ongoing fraud and misrepresentation. Commenting on the poll's findings, Jerry Jazinowski, the president of the National Association of Manufacturers, said, "Some companies get big, they get arrogant, and they lose touch with the community."[2]

Joseph E. Stiglitz, professor of economics at Columbia University, winner of the Nobel prize in economic science in 2001, and onetime head of the World Bank, suggests that the growing inequality of the rich and the poor brought on by globalization is a major cause of the rioting at meetings of the World Trade Center. He believes, too, that the violence is understandable and will increase as the disparity between the rich and poor continues to grow.[3]

News reports revealing that tobacco and chemical companies lied and covered up their own research reports on the dangers of their products along with award winning movies, such as *A Civil Action*, *John Q*, and *Erin Brockovich*, publicizing corporate lying and deception only fuel the expanding distrust and suspicion. And best-selling books, such as *Angry White Men*, contribute to the distrust of corporations.

Million dollar bonuses paid to executives at the expense of the general workers along with unanimous editorial disapproval by leading newspapers across the country have contributed to the public anger. And the Enron scandal only further inflamed the growing distrust of business. Pollster Daniel Yankelovich warns: "Executives haven't had to worry about social issues for a generation, but there's a yellow light flashing, now, and they better pay attention."[4]

In addition, the stakes are being raised. Failures and blunders in community relations may be embarrassing, but in the past they have often been short lived. The vilified *Exxon Valdez* oil spill, for example, caused momentary setbacks from organized boycotts of the company's products, yet the company's earnings have not suffered.

But the public is getting angrier and angrier with each new revelation of arrogant corporate behavior. Nothing, for example, is more central to the success of a pharmaceutical company than the protection of its patent rights. It protects research basic to product development for a pharmaceutical company. Pharmaceutical companies have strenuously resisted all efforts to alter this protection.

And they have been successful—that is until April 19, 2001, when thirty-nine major pharmaceutical companies were forced to give up their intellectual property rights in South Africa. This has set up a chain reaction putting patent rights under fire in other African nations, as well as Brazil and India.

Changing patent rights for drugs is on the agenda of WTO meetings. At the 2001 meeting in Qatar, agreement was reached despite the vigorous opposition of the pharmaceutical industry to give greater access to cut-rate drugs in poor nations by assuring that patent rules do not apply. The George W. Bush administration, over the wishes of the pharmaceutical industry, supported the WTO-negotiated trade agreement. We have no intention, said the U.S. Trade representative, of pursuing a trade policy that is "out of touch with our values."[5]

Activism and the support of activist causes go beyond corporations to affect governments and institutions. A group of Vietnam War veterans, fresh from forcing the American government to accept responsibility for the affects of Agent Orange on American soldiers, successfully persuade 122 nations, over the objections of the United States, to sign a treaty outlawing the use of land mines. In Boston, a group of Catholic parishioners, under the leadership of a Boston University business school professor, brought about the resignation of the Cardinal Archbishop, the first such event in the 2,000-year-old history of the Catholic Church.

We are in the midst of a worldwide revolution—an associational revolution as Lester Salamon, the head of Johns Hopkins Center for Civil Society Studies and a leading expert in what is now being called the third sector, prefers to call it.[6] And it is catching corporations flat-footed. The lessons are clear. Activism is increasing and becoming increasingly successful in determining what a company can or cannot do in communities and societies.

FAILURE OF COMMUNITY INVOLVEMENT

And how are companies responding to the new activism? Many, by doing more of the same. They jack up contributions, announce the start of a multimillion dollar charitable foundation, publicize their good works with glossy annual reports, buy half-page ads in newspapers and magazines publicizing their employee volunteer programs, underwrite public broadcasting programs, and expand their community and public affairs staffs.[7]

All to no avail. The public, according to studies conducted by companies themselves, knows very little about what a company donates to charities. And those that should know—public officials—are unimpressed. Some 100 mayors reported in a survey conducted by management consultants Sirota, Alper & Pfau that they were more concerned about the behavior of a company than its philanthropy. They ranked charitable contributions fifteenth among twenty-five attributes of performance they expected from a company. Heading the list were ethical corporate behavior, environmental protections, good treatment of customers, honest communication, and evenhanded government affairs.[8]

And the public is becoming increasingly suspicious of the motives of corporate community involvement. In a special edition of *Newsweek* magazine, examining the issues that will dominate the new millennium, the editors commented on the growth of corporate citizenship. Good deeds, *Newsweek* reported, along with doing well, were an emerging and growing new trend. While praising the new corporate social responsibility, the writers also ironically commented:

> But when no one's looking, corporations have a history of evading responsibility going back centuries. So if the business elite are going to be good citizens, the rest of us had better keep a close watch.[9]

And that was written before the Enron, WorldCom, Arthur Andersen, and Tyco scandals of 2002.

Even when a company is acting in what it believes is the best interests of a community, it can encounter unexpected opposition. In Connecticut, for example, corporations joined together to introduce legislation to reform the public education system. The reform, part of a larger national effort spearheaded by The Business Roundtable, a Washington, D.C., based organization of Fortune 100 CEOs, had the support of all the major Connecticut organizations and groups, including school administrators, and was a sure bet to be adopted. But it ran afoul of fundamentalist Christian groups who complained that the reform was too drastic and that it would put the school between the child and the family. The companies were accused of being anti-family. The legislation was withdrawn to avoid what appeared to be certain failure. The Business Roundtable, incidentally, has since abandoned its education reform strategy.

Lobbying public officials is also failing and even backfiring. Philip Morris was fined $75,000 for underreporting the amount of money it spent to lobby New York legislators.[10] Executives of Boston banks Fleet and Shawmut were labeled "stupid" by a business columnist of the *Boston Globe* for donating $10,000 to a pet charity of the chairman of the Massachusetts House Banking Committee in hopes he would kill a bill prohibiting banks from imposing ATM surcharges.[11] (He did.) Microsoft caused a firestorm of protest when it was discovered that the company lobbied Congress to defund the Justice Department when it had a case pending before the department's antitrust division.

And blaming the activists, a new tactic, is also not working. As colleges and governments discovered in the 1960s, calling activists and advocacy groups unrepresentative, elitist, and self-serving usually backfires. To claim, as Jack Welch, former CEO of the General Electric Company, that it was the actions of only a few environmental activists that prodded the federal government into actions that eventually forced the company to clean up the Hudson and Housatonic Rivers only misled the company and prevented it from finding solutions to the problems it faced.[12] It just generated more sympathy and ammunition for the activists.

THE NEW NORMS AND PRACTICES

We have entered into a new era in the relationship between companies and societies. Expectations are increasing. Tactics are becoming contentious and sometimes even violent. All the old rules and old practices that companies have depended on are being swept aside.

In other words, it's not about philanthropy. Equating philanthropy with corporate citizenship is the most common mistake CEOs make. In defending its environmental record, G.E.'s Jack Welch bragged to Charlie Rose on the *Charlie Rose Show* on April 17, 2001, about the company's generous contribution record. "That means we are a socially responsible company."

But it's not generosity, "It's the behavior, stupid," to modify a phrase used by President Clinton's public relations advisor, James Carville, whose mantra "It's the economy, stupid" is credited with contributing to the Clinton success in defeating the first George Bush in 1991.

Companies are now expected to safeguard the environment; support human rights; eliminate child labor; adopt codes of ethics; enter into partnerships with nongovernmental organizations (NGOs); display openness and transparency in relationships with customers, employees, community groups, and government organizations; promote diversity in the workplace; help communities solve their social problems; and consult with community residents on business plans and strategies.

These are the new rules that define the license of a company to operate. What happens to companies that do not adhere to the new rules? All the types of activist tactics described at the outset of the chapter—picketing, demonstrations, increased government regulation and oversight, boycotts, and blackmail.

A small but growing number of companies are learning how to operate under the new rules. They are developing strategies, programs, policies, and practices that emphasize new kinds of relationships. They are not interested in recapturing the business leadership position of the past but in changing the way their companies act and behave in an activist society. They are learning how to collaborate, how to create trust, how to achieve consensus with societies, communities, and activist groups as a way to participate in the process of defining the new business license to operate.

Example: Orin Smith, Starbucks CEO, volunteers alongside employees to clean beaches and develops programs to encourage customers to join with the company and volunteer in community projects.

Example: Shell and BP Oil companies announce that, unlike other oil companies and against the advice of President George W. Bush, they support adoption of the Kyoto protocol to reduce global warming.

Example: HP has a program to close the digital divide in communities as diverse as India, South Africa, and Palo Alto as part of its global social responsibility mission.

Example: Ford Motor Company funds programs to find solutions to the environmental effects of its manufacturing plants.

Example: IBM announces a major strategy to commit the company to bringing about public school reform and launches a worldwide volunteer program to bring technology to public education.

Example: Express Scripts, a pharmacy benefits company, announces in advertisements in major newspapers that it will provide a detailed disclosure of its sources of revenue and financial relationships with drug manufacturers as part of a seven-point "client pledge."

Example: General Electric makes corporate citizenship a major topic in its education of company managers.

Example: Fluor Corporation convenes all its senior managers to engage in a process of corporate citizenship strategy development.

Not all of these forward-looking companies are adopting the same strategies or practices. Not all are succeeding as well as they might. Some have only partial victories, but they are making progress. They are guided by five questions:

- Who are the external stakeholders in all our communities—local, regional, national, and global—that can influence our license to operate?

- What do they value?
- What are their concerns?
- What is the nature of our current relationships with these stakeholders?
- What is our stakeholder relations plan?[13]

That is the central message of this book. For a few managers, the trial of implementing corporate citizenship strategies is painful. But for most, at least for many described in this book, it is an exciting challenge. They see themselves as part of a new experiment, a new way of running a company in a world that is changing rapidly. It is a world that claims that the managerial capitalism of the past is old fashioned. It is a world that demands collaboration and cooperation. Those companies that understand this will prosper.

There is another message of this book.

A few companies are discovering that they can be change agents in improving the quality of discourse in communities and societies. In an era of contention, anger, and violence, some companies are serving as models for collaborative problem solving. They are able to give people encouragement and confidence to use consensus-seeking methods in bringing about peaceful social change in communities. The process, or the journey, in other words, has effects that go beyond the immediate experience in solving problems. It builds trust and it builds communities.

Of course there are those who differ with this conception of planning to bring about social change. Creating a more equitable society, they argue, can only occur by prodding, pushing, and pressuring companies and governments. Conflict strategies are the preferred method. Organizing groups is a tool to this end, to challenge social inequities and oppressive power.[14]

There are strong and persuasive arguments for conflict as a strategy for social change. It is often successful. The struggle for civil rights, the end to the Vietnam War, and even the recent protests at the World Trade Organization meetings are examples. But at what cost? Conflict is not too distant from violence, which itself is not at all too far from terrorism.

We need to bring about social change peacefully. It is part of our humankind progress to dignity and rationality. It is a message of this book, a message I would like to make to business leaders. Join with the few companies that are engaged in building a new collaborative society. Become part of a movement to build collaboration between business and society. Join with others in society to solve social and community problems, and forsake the power dominant business equation to change.

We are entering into a new era, an information age requiring conceivably new ways to work together. In a global society, power and information are shared widely.[15] Consensus methods for social change and community problem solving may not just be a method of choice but a method of necessity. Become part of this new venture.

CHAPTER 2

The Case for Change

This book took longer to write than originally planned. It wasn't because of other distractions or the lack of time. I had plenty of time. But what kept interfering is the exploding and relentless pace of change in corporate citizenship. And it is happening so quickly that it is becoming frustratingly difficult to chronicle.

Just think for a moment of the rate of change in the relationship between companies and societies since 1985. The modern era of corporate society and community relations began in the United States unintentionally when President Ronald Reagan decreased federal spending on health, social welfare, and education programs and then urged corporations to pick up the reductions by increasing donations to local charities. It was a welcome message to local charities and local governments. They began besieging companies—successfully, too— for donations.

In the United Kingdom, at around the same time, the Prince of Wales formed an organization called Business in the Community (BITC). Unlike President Reagan, Prince Charles used BITC as an advocacy organization to pressure the chief executive officers of companies in the United Kingdom and Europe to become socially involved in communities. Of course, the nonprofits, or nongovernmental organizations (NGOs) as they are now commonly called, caught the message just as their counterparts in the United States did and began looking to companies for grants and assistance.

Both actions came at a time when social activism was rising around the world. While President Reagan and Prince Charles were the emissaries of change, one unintentionally, the other very directly, the activists became the foot soldiers of change. Social activists are now major actors in defining a company's license to operate. It is a new world, a new society in which social activists, sophisticated and experienced, are demanding that companies exhibit new forms of behavior.

The change has been both swift and remarkable. What is driving it? What is forcing companies to adopt new rules of behavior in society? What, in other words, is the case for change?

There is not one driver but several that are helping to transform the way companies operate. The following are the most salient.

DISPERSED DECISION MAKING

One of the earliest drivers is the decentralization of decision making. Emerging in the United States during the Nixon years and culminating in the Reagan administration, the federal government as part of a tax saving effort and as a subtle way to fend off protests began shifting domestic programs to the states and local communities. States, many reluctantly, were forced to assume the responsibility for operating and supporting domestic programs.

As states began to assume responsibility for social programs, decision making became more and more dispersed. Suddenly, there were more "players" in the "game" of decision making, and they were considerably more sophisticated in knowing how to go about influencing political decisions, many of which began to have consequences for corporations.

States and communities began asserting their influence on corporate behavior in the 1970s. California, for example, passed emission control legislation more stringent than the federal government's. Automobile manufacturers discovered that they had to build cars to one set of expectations in one state and a different set of specifications in another state.

Local communities began passing other legislation that had consequences for corporations. Prohibiting smoking in businesses and public places is one example. Communities were also passing their own minimum wage legislation, setting up rules and regulations on working conditions and product safety, and holding companies responsible for consumer standards.

The newest influence in community decision making has been the rise of the global city. Cities that are moving into dominance in the global economy while the national economy declines in significance. The global city becomes the source of power in economies.

But the global city is also a source of power for the poor and dispossessed. Immigrants, women, African Americans in U.S. cities, and oppressed minorities, claims economist Joseph Stiglitz, are emerging as significant voices of influence in cities and local communities.[1]

What companies are learning is that they are becoming a part of the process of community decision making. When a company, for example, decides to expand a facility, move into a community, change an operating procedure, develop a community partnership, fund a charitable organization, pollute a stream, or enter into transnational activities, it is intervening in the process of community decision making. Not too long ago, business–government networks and relationships determined and governed the process. Opposition among these governing elite to community and civic ventures was rare. Business and government leaders shared the same backgrounds and beliefs, and they were able to anticipate each other's concerns and issues.

In those rare instances when opposition arose, it was frequently resolved quietly and amicably. A company president might be taken aside and "educated" on the position he (there never was a she) should take.[2] Solutions, of course, were made in the interests of a few, not the many. But the few always believed that, when they were acting in their own interests, they were acting in the best interests of the many.

Not so today. Under the new rules, there are many different resources that individuals or groups can use to influence the outcome of a decision. While it is still true that some individuals or organizations have more power by virtue of their position or resources, others, however, have learned how to create or combine a number of different influence resources to counter that power. Controlling votes, persistence, networking, community organizing, communication, publicity, and the use of expert knowledge are just a few of the resources that people now use to influence decisions.

No one resource dominates all the others in most, if not all, key decisions. Those who are successful in using the new rules of decision making rely on as many influence resources as they are capable of garnering.

It is also true that the tactics are different and messier than they once were. They may not be polite. Indeed, it may be confrontational, involving angry public meetings, picketing, boycotts, and occasionally even violence. These are all part of the new rules in the game of decision making—rules companies are now going to have to live with.

And the most important rule of all: Virtually no one, and certainly no group of more than a few individuals, is without some ability to obtain the resources and to create the sense of urgency needed to influence a decision.[3]

RISING CITIZEN ACTIVISM

Arguably, the most influential force of change has been the growth and sophistication of organized citizen advocacy. While it has long been popular to boast about the American tradition of voluntarism and citizen activism, beginning with Alexis de Tocqueville's observations a century ago, no one could have predicted the explosive growth and the wide diversity of citizen groups and nonprofit organizations that have emerged beginning in the 1960s.

The successes of the civil rights struggles and the student movements in universities and colleges, and then in the antiwar protests of the 1970s, jump-started the increase of a wide range of nonprofit organizations and citizen groups. All sorts of individuals, many who never even gave a thought to "fighting city hall," were organizing their friends, relatives, neighbors, fellow workers, colleagues, customers, and clients to solve social problems, press for the redress of wrongs, protest decisions, and promote public policies.

They were also establishing self-help groups, founding nonprofit organizations, setting up philanthropy foundations, and volunteering for citizen groups and charitable organizations. Citizen activism was on the rise, and it was having a profound effect on American society, changing the way governments, schools, and universities had to behave. By the 1990s, it was having an effect on the way corporations had to behave, too.

One reason for the success is the sheer volume of organizations that now exist. There are more than one million citizen organizations in India, 12,000 in Slovakia, 400,000 in Brazil and, according to the Urban Institute, 1.5 million in the United States, many of them recent. The number of nonprofits registered with the U.S. Internal Revenue Service increased 70 percent between 1989 and 1998. Aside from religious groups and foundations, 70 percent of the nonprofits filing returns with the IRS in 1998 were less than thirty years old. A third were less than fifteen years old.

Certainly, activism is not a primary function of every nonprofit organization. For some, like Greenpeace, it is, but for others, advocacy is one of a number of functions carried out in support of the organization's mission. The American Cancer Society, for example, raises money to sponsor research and to educate the public about the causes and cures of cancer, but it also conducts information campaigns to reduce smoking and lobbies governments to eliminate and outlaw cigarette smoking. The American Lung Association, formerly the TB Association, is a strong proponent of clean air legislation and a vocal critic of the George W. Bush administration's efforts to cut back on regulations governing emissions from coal-burning electric utility plants. And for still other nonprofit organizations, a specific issue may compel them to engage in advocacy activities to protect the purpose of the organization.

The historical society, for example, that stopped the Disney organization from moving into northern Virginia was a little known and not very powerful organization dedicated to the preservation of the character and history, particularly the Civil War history, of its community. It spurred the development of an activist group only because it believed the Disney Corporation was going to set up a park that would defame that history, despite company claims to the contrary.

There are also hundreds of other public interest organizations that are in business only to advocate for a cause or point of view. *Congressional Quarterly* and the Public Affairs Foundation list over 230 such advocacy organizations in its 1998–99 publication *Public Interest Profile*.[4]

There are also thousands of homeowners' associations, neighborhood "watch groups," and religious associations that potentially can affect the operations of a company. There is no way to estimate the numbers of these types of organizations or their success. We do know that they are becoming increasingly effective in forcing companies to change their plans. Mayors in many cities have set up bureaus to help businesses and citizen groups work together to resolve issues between businesses and neighbors.

In addition, and probably even a more significant development, are the hundreds, maybe even thousands, of spontaneous citizen groups that arise to protest the actions of a business and then disappear once the action is resolved. Neighbors in a working-class section of South Boston, Massachusetts, for example, organized to protest the building of a sports stadium in their area. Despite the support of the governor, media, sports fans, appointed public officials, and the spending of $4 million to promote the stadium, it was blocked. Other examples include the citizens that stop development of McDonald's restaurants, Wal-Mart stores, and the construction of cell towers. This kind of citizen activism is both ubiquitous and unpredictable.

Citizen activism is no longer an American phenomenon. It has grown to become a worldwide movement. Nongovernmental organizations around the world are growing at rates equal to the growth of those in the United States. In 1948, reports the Carnegie Endowment for International Peace, there were forty-one consulting groups accredited to the UN Economic and Social Council. Fifty years later, the number had grown to more than 1,500. Citizen organizations can now be found in such cities as Beijing, Moscow, Ankara, Jakarta, Manila, Durban, and Lima, and all are concerned about some aspect of the quality of life of their neighborhoods, cities, and countries.

But probably the bigger story in the success of citizen activism is its increased sophistication. Years of experience in participating or even observing the political protests of the past have shortened the learning curve. There are few if any individuals or groups of citizen that do not know how to develop a telephone calling tree, conduct a fundraising drive, write a press release, organize and publicize a protest, develop grant proposals, and make use of the old boy/old girl network to "get" to the influential decision maker or at the very least the gatekeepers to the decision makers.

Citizen groups and advocacy organizations have also developed their own self-help organizations. They have established networks, formed professional associations, set up training programs to teach community organizing skills, and run conferences that describe successful methods and tactics in communication and publicity. They publish journals and newsletters, set up Internet Web sites, and establish support groups for each other. Schools and universities teach courses and offer degrees in community organization. Law schools prepare lawyers for public interest law to promote advocacy goals.[5]

In addition, more and more college students are forsaking careers in business management for careers in running social agencies and public service organizations. They are volunteering for community nonprofits, many forsaking the annual spring break to build houses in poor neighborhoods for organizations like Habitat for Humanity.

Even business schools have added courses in nonprofit management. Harvard Business School, for example, established the John C. Whitehead Fund for Not-for-Profit Management—over, interestingly, the initial objections of many of the faculty—and introduced a program it calls the Initiative on Social Enterprise, complete with courses and internships in nonprofit agencies. In the first three years, enrollment increased 400 percent. A number of business schools—Columbia, Stanford, Duke, Yale, and Michigan, for example—have similar initiatives.

In short, citizen activism has become an integral part of the process in the way decisions are made in communities and societies. Over the past twenty years, governments have learned, sometimes painfully, to work with citizen groups and organizations. Now it is the corporations' turn to come to grips with the reality and force of citizen organizations. As a report from the Carnegie Foundation concludes, the issue is not whether to include citizen groups or NGOs in the deliberations and activities of companies. "The real challenge is figuring out how to incorporate them into corporate and governmental systems in ways that take account of their diversity and scope, their various strengths and weaknesses, and their capacity to disrupt as well as create."[6]

THE SELF-FULFILLMENT GENERATION

Underlying the growth and success of citizen groups has been a seismic generational shift in the publics' attitudes about the economy, catching both business leaders and politicians by surprise.

Until the 1970s, subsistence issues topped the list of public concerns—wages, employment, pensions, taxation, social security, agricultural subsidies, and job training. Not so today. The public, worldwide, is worried about the quality of life—environment, education, health care, personal security, and corporate behavior. We have entered, claims political scientist Jeffrey Berry, into what he calls a "post materialistic society" where there is less concern with lunch box issues and a growing concern for how we live.

Berry, whose study of federal legislation in three separate sessions of Congress between 1963 and 1991, led him to the conclusion that the debate had shifted. "In simple terms," said Berry, "policy decisions in Congress have moved from questions on how to increase the economic pie to questions about how to balance economic growth with the need to enhance the environment, protect consumers, or improve economic well-being."[7]

Berry's research also revealed that citizen groups were able to take advantage of this shift in attitudes to be able to successfully dominate the congressional policymaking process in a Republican pro business Congress. "Citizen groups," reports Berry, "were the primary political force that pushed the quality-of-life concerns on to the agenda of Congress." They became the antagonists to the business lobbies. "Over time," says Berry, "citizen groups were not only able to put their issues on the agenda but were able to get Congress to consider policies that are obnoxious to business and energetically fought by corporations and trade groups."[8]

Berry readily admits that his findings apply only to congressional decision making. But the evidence of the change is all too apparent. Communities reject the arguments of the past. Promises of jobs and increased money, for example, could not persuade the South Boston residents to accept a new stadium in their community. Nor could the Disney Company persuade the citizens of northern Virginia with promises of 12,000 new jobs and $1.68 billion in new taxes to support the building of its proposed theme park.

Increasingly, people no longer strive to seek needs that are related to what Abraham Maslow has described as physiological subsistence or self-subsistence. They seek to fulfill themselves. It is the "Q" factor, the quality of life that has become a prime motivator—clean and safe environment, access to education, guaranteed health care, and opportunities for personal growth and development.[9]

The self-fulfillment generation is also expressing its values in the marketplace. Grey Advertising calls them the "new age" consumers who use responsible community citizenship as a guide to buying.[10] Surveys and research reports back up Grey Advertising's observations. There is ever-increasing evidence that consumers are using the behavior of a company in making decisions about buying products.[11]

Nowhere, for example, is this transition to the self-fulfillment generation more dramatically demonstrated than in a five-year battle to reopen an oil pipeline from Houston, Texas, through Austin and El Paso to Arizona over strong and successful community opposition.

Twenty years ago, opposing the building of a pipeline in Texas would be unthinkable. Oil was king. Today, however, the high-tech industry now outranks oil in the state's gross product and in influence. And with that change has come a dramatic shift in attitudes. The former influential and powerful congressman from the El Paso district, J. J. Pickle, insists that what is stopping the pipeline is community concern with the environment and the quality of life. "It's not just that the oil industry has gotten weaker, but that the citizens and environmental groups have gotten so much stronger," said Pickle.[12]

Politicians, too, have misread the new shift in the public's attitudes. The most dramatic example is George W. Bush's loss to Senator John McCain in the 2000 New Hampshire presidential primary. The then governor of Texas, Bush campaigned on a pledge to reduce taxes, a popular promise in New Hampshire, the most anti-tax state in the United States. But the voters surprised him. They were more interested in his proposals on education, health care, and the solvency of Social Security. Bush was unprepared for this shift, leaving him unable to respond quickly enough to save his New Hampshire primary. He subsequently shifted to promoting self-fulfillment issues, such as education, and rescued his campaign for the presidency.

GLOBALIZATION—TURNING COMPANIES AND COMMUNITIES INTO STRANGERS . . .

On June 7, 1999, The CEO of Minneapolis-based Honeywell Corporation, Michael Bonsignore, shocked the twin cities of Minneapolis and St. Paul by announcing the company was merging with Allied Signal Company and moving its corporate headquarters to Morristown, New Jersey.

Begun in 1885 as the Minneapolis Heat Register Company, then the Minneapolis-Honeywell Regulator Company in 1927, and finally just Honeywell in 1964, it was the national icon of a loyal corporate citizen. Honeywell was universally admired, and companies everywhere copied its programs and followed its lead.

Here are just a few of the contributions Honeywell had made to the twin cities prior to the merger:

- Made volunteerism a requirement for senior executives, and provided time off for employees for their volunteer work.
- Set up a retiree volunteer program.
- Established a high school in its headquarters site for pregnant and teenage mothers.
- Avoided moving its plant site from a low-income inner city neighborhood to the suburbs by partnering with Habitat for Humanity to build over fifty homes for residents. Thousands of employees volunteered to participate in the project. Honeywell donated over $4.8 million.
- During the Vietnam War, the company was regularly picketed and condemned by peace groups. Police had to use clubs and mace to clear protestors outside the company's 1970 annual meeting. In response,

Honeywell organized a peace conference in collaboration with the Humphrey School of Public Affairs of the University of Minnesota. In an environment of protest, it was a risky decision. The gamble, however, paid off. It muted the protests and brought considerable praise from the media and national policy leaders.

* Developed a novel program for children and young families called Success by Six, which has since become a signature program of local United Ways across the country.

Losing such commitment to the community was devastating. The mayor, a close friend of Bonsignore, was shocked. He learned about the decision the evening before it was made and was told there was no opportunity for officials to try to change Honeywell's mind.

Peter McLaughlin, a county board member who worked closely with Honeywell in rebuilding the south Minneapolis area, expressed his disappointment, "[W]e're being victimized by larger corporate powers over which we have no control. To lose that capacity is a huge loss for the community."

McLaughlin's comments came before a second bombshell was dropped on the twin cities. On October 27, 2000, Bonsignore returned to Minneapolis to dedicate the Honeywell-built housing complex in the Phillips neighborhood near the company's headquarters. On the same day, an announcement was made in Fairfield, Connecticut, by the General Electric Company. It was buying the Honeywell Company.

And then in July 2001, a third bombshell, the European Commission, blocked General Electric's proposed $45 billion takeover of the Honeywell Company to the surprise and chagrin of G.E.'s CEO Jack Welch. Bonsignore resigned and Lawrence Bossidy, former CEO of Allied Signal, was appointed CEO of Honeywell.

Although the Honeywell story may be more convoluted, it is now an all too familiar story in communities everywhere. The Boeing Company shocked its hometown of Seattle in March 2001 by announcing it was moving its headquarters from Seattle, where the company was founded by William Boeing in 1916, to Chicago. The Hoover Company, once a major employer in Canton, Ohio, has been sold twice and is now owned by Maytag. Sohio became a subsidiary of British Petroleum that later also bought Amoco and changed its name to BPAmoco. Burger King was acquired by a giant food company in London called Grand Metropolitan, which changed its name to Diageo after it bought Guinness, the Irish beer company. Zebco Corporation, the inventor of the spin cast fishing reel and a symbol of Americanism, closed its production line and moved it to China.

In each of these instances, the companies insisted that they would continue to maintain their level of commitment to the community. All too often, however, the opposite is true. "Shifts to absentee ownership," explains Marina v.N. Whitman, Harvard Business School professor and former vice president of General Motors, "have often meant reduction or total elimination of jobs in the company's original community as local operations are downsized, moved, or simply closed down. But even when jobs have stayed put," continues Whitman, "the company's role in the community, and that of its management, has almost inevitably changed. An executive who heads what is now a division of a larger company headquartered elsewhere is unlikely to have the same motivation—or the same leeway—to use resources for the gain-sharing and community leadership that once characterized good corporations."[13]

Communities around the world are left without the corporate leadership that once was used to build the nonprofit sector. And they are left without the leadership to facilitate the transfer to a global economy. Little wonder why the alienation of the public to companies is growing.

... AND RAISING FEARS AND ANXIETIES AROUND THE WORLD

Globalization has also become a political issue, raising fears and anxieties around the world. Fears of globalization, warranted or unwarranted, changed the agenda of the World Trade Organization and the World Bank. It forced President Clinton to modify his stance on the merits of globalization and dominated the discussions at the January 2000 meeting of the World Economic Forum in Davos, Switzerland. Meetings of these organizations continue to cause protests and demonstrations wherever they are held.

In the United States, for example, it has become the antibusiness rallying cry of the twenty-first century, uniting the Left and the Right—Ralph Nader and Pat Buchanan, for example, both campaigned for the presidency in 1999 on an antiglobalization agenda. While neither was successful, their campaigns struck responsive chords among the public.

And offshore outsourcing, a product of globalization, became the economic touchstone of the campaign for the presidency in 2004.

Massachusetts Senator John Kerry and President George W. Bush each tried to outdo the other in claiming they would curtail the growth of globalization, despite the efforts of American businesses to dissuade them to do otherwise.

The erosion of manufacturing jobs to China—dozens in companies in California, alone, for example, are moving manufacturing jobs to China each month—is making globalization the major social issue of the decade of the new millennium. The movement of manufacturing jobs to China and service jobs to India will continue to grow and consume the energy and time of business leaders everywhere.

"The more citizens begin to feel that in this new system of globalization things are controlled from afar, not from at home, the more the globalizers in these countries will be exposed to attacks," claims *New York Times* columnist Thomas Friedman. "Clearly," he adds, "one of the biggest challenges for political theory in this globalization era is how to give citizens a sense that they can exercise their will, not only over their own governments but over at least some of the global forces [read corporations] that are shaping their lives."[14]

THE RISING POWER OF THE INTERNET

It took thirty-eight years for the radio to reach 50 million users.
It took the personal computer sixteen years to reach the same number of users.
It took the World Wide Web only four years.[15]

Thirty years ago when anyone walked into the office of a nongovernmental organization, he or she heard the whirring sound of a mimeograph machine churning out two or three dozen notices of an upcoming meeting. Fifteen years later, it was the swish, swish, swishing sound of a copying machine making it possible to mail out hundreds of announcements of a community meeting or to send alerts to media contacts statewide. Today, the click of a mouse allows a citizen group to e-mail thousands of contacts anywhere in the world within seconds.

The Internet:

• Was the principal strategy used by a group of Vietnam War veterans to successfully persuade nations to outlaw the use of land mines;
• Helped Greenpeace to garner instant support for its successful opposition to Shell's decision to dispose of a used oil rig in the North Atlantic;

- Is where the Sierra Club's ten tips for boycotting an oil company can be found on its Web pages;
- Was the way a couple in Marietta, Georgia, forced the Ford Motor Company to announce the largest recall in the automobile industry—the cost to the company was estimated to be $200 to $300 million;
- Is the source for reading about worst-case chemical scenarios to alert communities of the danger of chemical hazards;
- Used by retired General Perry Smith to force CNN/Time Warner to issue an apology for erroneously reporting on the use of chemical weapons during the Vietnam War;
- Is the way members of the outlawed Falun Gong are informed to assemble in Tiananmen Square in China;
- Is the means that neighborhood organizations, such as the almost 2,000 neighborhoods in Denver, Colorado, use to alert neighbors of neighborhood-related issues and announce community meetings.

No government, no organization, and no company is immune from the organizing potential of the Internet. "There is," comments an activist in Brazil to *New York Times* columnist Thomas Friedman, "no hiding place anymore for bad corporate behavior in a globally interconnected activism."[16]

The Internet, in other words, has become the wild card and the new dynamic in the shift of forces affecting the stakeholder relationships between companies and communities. It is easier, faster, and cheaper than any other community organizing technique. It has changed the power equation. Protests can be organized, publicity campaigns initiated, boycotts started, and supporters notified of emergency meetings instantaneously.

THE BOOMERS INHERIT THE CORNER OFFICE

In 1994, a group of employees of Interface Company, a mid-sized manufacturer of carpeting and floor tiles, asked CEO Ray Anderson to talk about the company's environmental vision. Unprepared because the company did not have a vision, Anderson read *The Ecology of Commerce* given to him by a friend. It was an epiphany. He became a vocal and ardent supporter of environmental sustainability, claiming that his company had "a moral duty to transform itself into an ecologically sustainable operation."[17]

In an earlier era, every community had its corporate civic champion. In Boston, it was Charles Francis Adams, Raytheon CEO and descendant of two presidents, who was the leading spark for the Boston

United Way. David Packard, of Hewlett-Packard, was the philanthropic and community leader in Santa Clara, whose contributions, energies, and civic advocacy led to the birth of the Silicon Valley. Cleveland had John Greene of Ohio Bell Telephone as a much heralded community leader. This was the era of managerial capitalism when companies tolerated a host of company objectives besides shareholder value.[18]

Beginning in the 1980s, CEOs in the United States began drifting away from personal involvement in community affairs. They turned over philanthropy to staffs—administrative secretaries, public relations personnel, and a new type of manager, the community relations professional.

The CEOs retreated into the background, much to the dismay of community groups and nonprofit organizations. In mid 1980s, the Council on Foundations, for example, commissioned pollster Daniel Yankelovich to study the attitudes of CEOs toward philanthropy. Most of the then "current" CEOs agreed that companies had an obligation to be involved in local charities. Future CEOs, those ready to take over the mantle of running companies, however, were less likely to be involved or believe that community involvement was important.

A third of the next generation CEOs were not involved. The median hours they spent on community involvement was 2.9. For the then current CEOs, the median time was 4.0 hours. Some nine out of ten next-generation CEOs claimed that the then harsh business environment was an obstacle to corporate charity. Only half of the then current CEOs expressed this attitude. The future CEOs also insisted that corporate giving had to support the company's business goals.[19]

But a new trend began emerging in the latter part of the 1990s. CEOs and directors of companies who are products of the activist 1960s began raising issues of environmental sustainability and corporate social responsibility. Lord John Browne, CEO of BP, announces support for the Kyoto Protocol to reduce global warming. William Clay Ford, chairman of Ford Motor Company, admits that the SUVs they manufacture are harming the environment. Ben Cohen and Jerry Greenfield, founders of Ben & Jerry's Ice Cream, became national icons for promoting corporate social responsibility. Arnold Hiatt, former president and CEO of the Stride Rite Corporation, received widespread national press for making corporate citizenship a hallmark of his company's mission.

This new breed of "social visionary"[20] CEO is moving into the corner office. Despite criticism from their business colleagues, they insist on promoting employee voluntarism, conserving energy, demanding ethical behavior, and speaking out in support of government initiatives and policies on environmental sustainability.

Many joined with Business for Social Responsibility (BSR), an organization once composed of small businesses, activists, and policy wonks, to promote corporate social responsibility. Under the leadership of Arnold Hiatt and BSR CEO Robert Davis, former director of the Levi Strauss Foundation, BSR has evolved into a worldwide organization promoting business decision–making linked to ethical values and respect for people, communities, and the environment. Hiatt and Davis retired in 2004. Both remain on the BSR board.

In Europe, the shift has been driven by the Prince of Wales in Great Britain. Using organizations he founded in 1985, Business in the Community and the Leadership Forum, Prince Charles has been able to convince European business leaders that corporate responsibility is an essential business practice.

FEDERALIZING THE SOCIAL BEHAVIOR OF COMPANIES

Regulating the social and environmental behavior of companies is not new, but demanding that companies must consult with citizen committees is. This is one of the fastest growing trends in the relationship of companies to societies, and the one least written about.

One form of governing the behavior of companies is to set standards for their performance in the community or society. There are a growing number of standards, too many according to some critics, that are being used to evaluate a company's social and environmental behavior and practices. The CERES principles for environmental stewardship is one example. It is used as criteria for investors and others to assess the environmental performance of companies.

Another example is The Standards of Excellence published by The Center for Corporate Citizenship at Boston College (see Table 2.1). Developed by a committee of The Center's International Advisory Board, its purpose is to serve as a self-study method for a company to evaluate its own performance.

In practice, community consultation over issues and concerns is not new. Many oil and chemical companies have community advisory panels (CAPs) composed of citizens that serve as a liaison between the company and the community. CAPs provide a structure for addressing

Table 2.1
The Standards of Excellence*

    I. **Leadership:** Top level executives demonstrate support, commitment, and participation in community involvement efforts.

   II. **Issues Management:** The company identifies and monitors issues important to its operations and reputation.

 III. **Relationship Building:** Company management recognizes that building and maintaining relationships of trust with the community is a critical component of company strategy and operations.

 IV. **Strategy:** The company develops a strategic plan for community programs and responses that is based on mutual issues, goals, and concerns of the company and community.

  V. **Accountability:** All levels of the organization have specific roles and responsibilities for meeting community involvement objectives.

 VI. **Infrastructure:** The company incorporates systems and policies to support, communicate, and institutionalize community involvement objectives.

VII. **Measurement:** The company establishes an ongoing process for evaluating community involvement strategies, activities and programs, and their impact on the company and community.

---

*Trademarked by The Center for Corporate Citizenship at Boston College.

community concerns. They are not infrequently used to provide an advocacy voice for the company in the community.

Community consultation can also arise as a consequence of disputes or issues of concern about the current or potential operations of a company. There are dozens of examples listed in the previous chapter describing disputes between companies and communities that eventually forced companies to collaborate with a citizen group. Most managers are unprepared for spontaneous consultation with a community citizen group that is often carried out under the glare of widespread media coverage.

The trend toward government oversight of corporate citizenship has not been fully played out, but it is on the way. In some countries, Canada and Ireland for example, companies are required to work with committees if the development actions of the company have community implications. Mayors of many cities in the United States insist that development companies obtain community acceptance as part of a permitting process. The acceptance is often based on how many amenities a developer will provide to the community to "mitigate" the negative impacts of the development project.[21] Efforts to require community consultation on environmental issues have been introduced into the legislature in Minnesota.

In the United Kingdom, the Company Responsibilities Bill has been introduced in Parliament. The bill sets up four requirements:

1. making environmental and social reporting mandatory;
2. requiring directors to consider environmental and social impacts, making them liable if they are negligent in failing to do so;
3. creating a Corporate Responsibility Board to do investigations and conduct random audits; and
4. establishing multiple penalties, including imprisonment, fines, suspension from stock exchanges, or suspension of operations.[22]

In Canada, the Bank Act requires reporting on community involvement practices. In Australia, the top 1,000 companies are required to produce a report on the impact of the company on communities.

It is very likely that in the near future, companies will be hiring community negotiators just as they hired labor negotiators when workers became organized. In fact, just such a prediction was announced by Stanley Allyn, chairman of the National Cash Register Company. Speaking to a business group Allyn said, "Industry's responsibility to the community can be met practically and profitably. Delay in assuming this obligation is dangerous. We have a costly and formidable lesson in labor relations. The consequence of years of indecision is a Federal mandate to curb and control. History may repeat itself with the corporation in its relation to the community."[23] That prediction was made in the 1950s.

SUMMARY

It is unmistakably clear that the forces dictating how a company can operate in communities and societies are changing, and they will continue to change because they are based on emerging *social* expectations. The era of economic uncertainty appears to be over. The major concern of people worldwide is improving the quality of their life now and in the future. And the public looks to a vastly growing group of activist organizations to ensure that the new social expectations are fulfilled.

CHAPTER 3

The Faces of Activism

THE MATTAPOISETT CELL TOWER

The news got around quickly. A cell tower was going to be built in the Hollywoods section of Mattapoisett, Massachusetts.

Jo Pannell, a retired social worker, whose property was adjacent to the land selected for the cell tower, was the first to sound the alarm. Pannell is on the board of the local library and the historical commission, is active in the parish Catholic Church, and is personally friendly with many town officials through her volunteer work. She is, as one town official put it, an effective activist in the best sense of that word for the town.

On hearing the news, she immediately contacted the zoning board. The tower, they explained, was proposed by AT&T to meet the exploding use of cell phones and pagers in southeastern Massachusetts. It would be built on a small portion of some thirty acres of mostly wetland bordering Aucoot and Hollywoods Roads, owned by Charles T. Boardman, a former resident of Mattapoisett and now living in Utah. Boardman had inherited the land from his father, one of the original settlers of the Hollywoods section, over 100 years ago. The thirty acres were all that remained of hundreds of acres the Boardmans once owned and had sold over the years parcel by parcel.

Dwellings could not be built on the thirty acres because of wetland requirements. A small portion of the thirty acres, however, could support the building of a cell tower and a small maintenance building.

Federal law, explained the town planner, requires that municipalities set aside land designated for cell towers. Most communities designate land distant from residential sections. Mattapoisett had done the same and chosen a strip of land adjacent to interstate route 195 on the northern edge of the town.

A waiver, however, can be granted by a municipality to permit building cell towers outside the designated site. AT&T was requesting such a waiver. A hearing on the waiver was planned for December 18, 2002.

Hollywoods is a residential section of Mattapoisett, located on the shore of Buzzards Bay near the entrance to the Cape Cod Canal. It is a mixed neighborhood containing modest homes of year-round residents, summer cottages, and a growing number of million dollar vacation homes of professionals and business executives.

Pannell sent notices to her neighbors warning them of the proposed tower. She recruited some half-dozen neighbors, who were equally upset about the Boardman proposal. They helped to distribute notices and make calls to the residents. She posted a large sign on the main road leading through Hollywoods announcing the cell tower proposal and notifying residents of the town meetings to discuss the waiver request.

Copies of the waiver proposal were distributed by Pannell's small group. Pannell was a constant visitor to the town hall to stay abreast of the tower proposal. She and most of the residents distrusted the town planning process. They believed that Boardman and his lawyers had the power and skills to overwhelm the process.

This distrust was given apparent credence when the meeting scheduled for the hearing was postponed. The local scuttlebutt was that it was a trick, a big business trick. Boardman was trying to circumvent the process and seek a resolution privately. In truth, the reason for the postponement was that Boardman's lawyer had a scheduling conflict.

Pannell changed the sign announcing the new meeting date. Her group got on the phone and notified the area residents of the rescheduled date.

The hearing on the waiver request was scheduled in Mattapoisett's town hall, a two-story Cape Cod–style shingle building built in 1896. The room for the meeting was approximately fifteen feet by twenty-five feet, large enough to accommodate the five members of the zoning board, secretary, town planner, and twenty-five to thirty observers. Rarely did zoning board meetings attract more than a handful. But on this date, the room was filled to overflowing; some fifty to sixty residents showed up. People stood along the walls and the back of the room. Many, unable to get into the meeting room, lined the hallway outside the meeting room.

Boardman, not present, was represented by a lawyer, who claimed that the tower was needed to meet the growing use of pagers, cell phones, and wireless computers. He said that to deny Boardman the right to use the land for a cell tower was unfair. He paid taxes on land he was unable to build on. The only use for the land could be a cell tower.

The residents began their presentations. Dana Coggin, a retired lawyer, made a short presentation and distributed copies of a letter to the zoning board outlining the reasons for the group's objections. There was, said Coggin, no demonstrable proof that the tower was needed. A cell tower adjacent to the interstate already existed. Building a cell tower in a residential neighborhood would be unsightly and could cause the value of the houses in the area to become depressed.

A letter from a high-technology businessman, not present because of scheduling conflicts, was read suggesting that the cell tower may have health and environmental consequences that had not been addressed in the proposal. Further study, he recommended, is needed to address the health consequences.

Dozens of other residents commented, claiming that the tower would decrease land values and alter the unique aesthetics of a beach community. The zoning board members were becoming visibly uncomfortable at this point. A final comment came from one resident that seemed to sum up the residents' personal objections: "Mr. Boardman's father would never have proposed that a cell tower be built on his land. It would be like erecting a bill board on Hollywoods Road."

The zoning board first suggested delaying a decision to allow the planning commission time to study the waiver requests. This was met with strong and quick objections. Except for Boardman and his lawyer, everyone was opposed to the cell tower, the residents insisted. Why delay making a decision when all the residents opposed it.

The zoning board quickly folded. The waiver was denied unanimously.

THE WOMEN OF UGBORODO

In the early morning hours of July 8, 2002, hundreds of women, defying all tradition, began a protest and occupation of Chevron/ Texaco's Escravos Terminal in Nigeria across the river from their village of Ugborodo. For ten days, the women, led by village store owner Alicia Atsepoyi, occupied the offices of the terminal refusing to leave until their demands were met. The occupation garnered worldwide press coverage, including a photograph of the women standing on the docks preventing workers from entering the terminal.

As the owner of a small store, Mama Ayo, as Ms. Atsepoyi is commonly called, knows everyone in the village. She sits in front of her store greeting passersby and chatting with customers. There is little in the village that Mama Ayo does not know.

All that she and her neighbors were asking for was community development, schools, and jobs.

For over forty years, Chevron had been operating the Escravos Terminal, shipping billions of dollars worth of oil to the United States. For over forty years, the poor small fishing village of Ugborodo sank further and further into abject poverty. In fact, the village itself was actually sinking into the water, attributed in part to the company's actions in widening the creak and nearby river. Outhouses made of corrugated zinc are built along the river, discharging effluents into the water where the residents fish for crabs. Schools are almost nonexistent. Medical facilities are primitive and in sharp contrast to the employee medical facilities of the Chevron/Texaco terminal.

The Chevron Company had not deliberately neglected the village of Ugborodo. Of the money Chevron gives to an African government, 40 percent of the oil revenue goes to Chevron and 60 percent to the government, ostensibly for national and community development. Little of the 60 percent, however, gets back to the residents because of widespread corruption. Chevron/Texaco managers insist that there is little the company can do. Corruption is a way of life in Nigeria.

Chevron has also donated money for economic development—some $36 million—according to Chevron executives. But there is little to show for it. Much of the money is siphoned off by corrupt officials. Chevron executives shrug their shoulders in frustration.

Violence in the late 1990s forced oil companies to hire "community liaison officers" to act as go-betweens with rulers of small Nigerian communities. It is essentially protection money and obviously another form of corruption.

None of this is explainable or understandable to the residents. All they know is that the company is making millions of dollars from their country's natural resources and returning nothing to the community. The distrust festers and grows against the large American company.

While the occupation was taking place, Chevron executives were attending a meeting in London. Production in the Escravos Terminal ground to a halt. Employees were reluctant to confront the protestors or eject them from the facility. The women protestors were becoming increasingly stronger in their demands.

Chevron executives abruptly adjourned their meeting and rushed back to Nigeria to begin negotiations in a town hall built by Shell. At the meeting, Chevron/Texaco executives detailed all that the company was doing for the village—a generator, water tank, a primary school.

Undeterred, the villagers said that was not enough. While the executives of the company lived in comparative luxury, the villagers were living in misery. They demanded 100 jobs, new roads, 500 two-room houses, and embankments to stop the river erosion. The company agreed in a memorandum of understanding to provide electricity and water to the community directly from the terminal facilities and to build a school, a community center, and houses for community elders. It also agreed to help the women set up poultry and fish farms.

From Chevron/Texaco's point of view, the issue in Nigeria is a no-win situation. "We can't take the place of government," insists David J. O'Reilly, the CEO. It's unrealistic. It's not our role. But the worst thing we could do is nothing."[1]

The women of Ugborodo are hopeful. Mama Ayo believes the company will honor its commitment. Americans, she says, are not bad people.

THE ORGANIZED ACTIVISTS: GREENPEACE AND BRENT SPAR

The pictures in both British and American newspapers and news magazines and on television captured a moment of high drama. On June 10, 1995, Greenpeace activists in small boats circled around a Shell U.K. oil rig named the Brent Spar that was being towed out to be sunk 150 miles off the coast of Scotland in the North Sea. A few activists were pictured scrambling around the rig posting notices claiming that Shell was about to cause an environmental disaster.

Shell's deepwater disposal decision was not arrived at hastily. It was a decision based on four years of planning and study. Observations by scientists (including a Nobel Prize winner), consultants, and university researchers concluded that sinking the rig in the Atlantic Ocean was a sound environmental decision. From an environmental perspective, explained the researchers, disposing of the rig in the ocean was more environmentally advisable than getting rid of it on dry land. Government officials agreed with Shell officials. All pertinent regulators supported Shell. Elected officials, including John Major, the prime minister, approved and supported the plan. But Greenpeace activists disagreed. They contended that millions of gallons of oil still in the rig would be emptied in the sea along with corrosive steel causing untold ecological damage.

They issued a call to action of its members. They sent thousands of e-mails to successfully organize opposition to Shell's plans. They called for a boycott of Shell products. Their actions resulted in vandalizing and firebombing of gas stations and a 50 percent drop of sales in Germany in a matter of weeks.

Greenpeace said it opposed the violence that occurred. Its mission, it claims, is to use nonviolent, creative confrontation to expose global environmental problems and force solutions for a green and peaceful future. It finances its research and activist program through voluntary contributions and membership dues. It refuses to accept government funds or contributions from foundations that do not agree with the organization's mission.

Greenpeace conducts activist campaigns for

1. the protection of ocean and ancient forests;
2. to phase out of fossil fuels and to promote renewable energy to stop climate change;
3. to eliminate toxic chemicals;
4. to prevent genetically modified organisms from being released into nature; and
5. for safe and sustainable trade.[2]

Ten days after it began towing the rig, Shell had to admit defeat and rescind its plan. The rig was moved to a Norwegian fjord.

To surrender to the activists was a devastating blow to Shell. It was costly. Employee morale plummeted. Commenting on the event, Heinz Rotheremund, managing director of Shell U.K., said, "Brent Spar will go down in history as an icon—as a symbol of the inability of large corporations to engage in meaningful dialogue with stakeholders."[3]

BUSINESS IN THE COMMUNITY

In 1982, the Prince of Wales founded an organization named Business in the Community (BITC) to promote business involvement in the community. Businesses, he explained, had an obligation to support the social and economic needs of community, not just for the needs of the community but also in their own self-interest. Studies and reports, many of which were supported by funds from BITC, revealed that consumers and employees strongly endorsed involvement of companies in communities.

Prince Charles's support of BITC would benefit local communities, but he forecasted that it would also provide a competitive advantage for U.K. companies in the expanding European Common Market. It is an interesting concept yet to be proved. But it does seem to be aligned to more and more studies claiming that there is a business reason for corporate community involvement.

It is as an activist that Prince Charles has been most successful. He has been able to persuade U.K. companies to endorse and accept the new corporate citizenship, making many companies in the United Kingdom leaders in corporate citizenship. And he has done it in a unique way—persuasion.

One program he started was called "Seeing Is Believing." Beginning in 1992, he asked CEOs to spend a day observing the work of a community organization—school, halfway house, reformatory, health clinic, AIDS agency, settlement house, or organizations for abused children and spouses, for example. All visits are required to be scheduled during a particular month.

After their visits, CEOs are invited to a meeting and luncheon at St. James Palace, a truly impressive meeting site adjacent to Green Park. Gathered in tables of eight to ten, the CEOs prepare a report on their observations and recommendations for corporate roles in the community. The Prince responds to each of the reports and uses their observations as a vehicle to promote corporate citizenship.

In response to questions from the Prince, the CEOs say that the visits were valuable. They learned about their communities and the value of corporate involvement in community affairs. Of course, many of the responses are given to please the Prince, according to some cynics. They say privately that few of the CEOs fulfilled the day in the agency; most spent only half a day and some an hour or two.

Nonetheless, the program, along with other programs of BITC, has been successful in changing the attitudes of CEOs to community involvement. Since it began, over 3,000 senior executives in the United Kingdom visited inner-city programs and initiatives. An average of 100 executives are engaged in the Seeing Is Believing program each year. They have also produced programmatic results. In 1994, for example, a group of companies set up a mentoring program called "Roots and Wings" for people interested in setting up a small business. A major television company uses a series of programs to encourage companies to accept challenges from community groups.[4]

Is it a stretch to call the Prince of Wales an activist? Is he comparable to Jo Pannell or the Greenpeace volunteers or Mama Ayo?

Few U.S. companies have made as much progress toward adopting corporate citizenship practices as companies in the United Kingdom. The triple bottom line—profits, societal concerns, and environmental sustainability—has become a popular mission of many U.K. companies. The Prince of Wales has used his charisma and positional legitimacy to promote a cause. And he has achieved amazing success.

THE CYBER ACTIVISTS

On a November morning just before Thanksgiving 1994, Andy Grove, the president and CEO of Intel Corporation, received a call from his communications director asking for an urgent meeting. Reporters from CNN, he was told, were on the way to the company's headquarters to film a story on the company's refusal to replace a faulty Pentium processor chip that Intel's customers had installed in their computers.

Intel was alerted to the problem of the processor chip by a mathematician shortly after the chip was manufactured. The company conducted its own analysis and concluded that the flaw was minor, affecting only those doing complex math division problems. It was estimated that the average spreadsheet user would run into a problem caused by the faulty chip every 27,000 years. There was no need to replace the chip except for those very rare instances when users could demonstrate they were engaged in sophisticated math division problems.

News of Intel's decision began circulating first on the Internet. Then trade papers began picking up on the story, followed shortly by the CNN television report, and finally newspapers and television stations across the country. It was national news, and Intel was under heavy criticism by the media and computer users to change its policy. Intel refused.

But then came the IBM announcement. It was halting shipment of computers containing the Pentium processor. At this point, according to Grove, "All Hell broke loose." Customers were calling in and complaining. Employees were getting inquiries from neighbors, friends, and family. Morale at Intel was sinking fast.

"After a number of days of struggling against the tide of public opinion dealing with the phone calls and the abusive editorials, it became clear that we had to make a major change," said Grove.

In December 1994, less than a month since CNN first reported on the faulty processor, Intel backtracked and changed its policy. Anyone, regardless of what level of statistical analysis he or she was doing, could call in and get a replacement chip. An entirely new division was created just to handle the replacement calls. Hundreds of thousands of chips were replaced, along with thousands of technical help calls to assist people who did not know how to replace the chips.

The company took a hit of $475 million, the equivalent of half a year of its R&D budget, or five years of advertising costs of the Pentium chip.

THE COMMITTEE FOR RESPONSIVE PHILANTHROPY

The major charitable and civic event in communities all across the United States, from the 1940s through the late 1980s, was the annual Community Chest or United Fund drive for the support of local charities. It was advertised as a single campaign for a community's voluntary health, welfare, and recreation agencies. Allocation of the funds raised to the local agencies was made on the basis of a citizen budget review of needs. In this way, all agencies were treated in the same way, regardless of popularity or emotional appeal.

For business and industry, the annual campaign, now called the United Way, was a perfect answer for meeting charitable requests from a growing number of local agencies. Consequently, companies deferred their giving practices to the United Way and gave it the exclusive right to solicit charitable contributions from employees. Trade union officials also supported the United Way's annual campaign, many customarily serving along with corporate executives on United Way committees. Payroll deduction methods were established to make giving easier for employees. Employees were urged to donate one hour's pay a month to the annual drive. Executives were asked to make their contributions based on a percentage of their annual salary, a percentage that was devised by United Way committees.

Employee or workplace giving was a major factor in the growth and success of United Way. Close to 70 percent of all money raised by United Way during that period came from corporate gifts and employee donations. The old-fashioned door-to-door fund-raising tactic gave way to the more efficient and lucrative workplace campaigns.

Beginning in the 1980s, the United Way came under fire for its "monopolistic" practices. New charities serving minorities and women were consistently turned down for membership in the United Way and, thus, unable to participate in the annual community fund drive.

An incident in Philadelphia publicized United Way's monopoly. Under pressure from the Catholic cardinal archbishop, the United Way turned down membership for a women's organization that, among other services, provided abortion and contraceptive counseling. The decision created a furor. Hundreds of donors refused to support the United Way and sent their contributions directly to the women's organization.

The "new wave" organizations were also shut out from conducting their own workplace campaigns. Companies customarily signed charter agreements that gave the United Way exclusive rights to campaign for funds from employees.

In 1985, activist Robert Bothwell organized the new wave charities and their sympathizers to challenge United Way's monopoly under the banner of the National Committee for Responsive Philanthropy. The United Way, claimed Bothwell, was a business-dominated organization. Only agencies that met the favor of community business leaders could become members of the United Way. It should, said one critic, be legislated out of existence.[5] The president of the new and up-and-coming trade union for government employees, AFSCME, called the United Way "charity OPEC."

Dismissed as a nuisance, Bothwell and his National Committee for Responsive Philanthropy persisted. They recruited other activists and organizations to join their cause: Native American Rights Fund; the Center for Community Change; The Grey Panthers; Women's Way, USA; the National Council of La Raza; Environmental Support Group; Asian American Defense and Education Fund; Consumer Federation of America; Urban Coalition Jewish Community Services; United Latino Fund; and the Black United Fund were affiliated and supported the cause of the National Committee for Responsive Philanthropy.

In contrast, the United Way of America's board consisted of the business world's cream of the crop. Serving on the board of United Way of America were the CEOs of dozens of Fortune 100 companies, including Johnson & Johnson, Prudential Insurance Company, American Express, IBM, General Electric, AT&T, United Airlines, Quaker Oats, J.C. Penney, Sears, and Raytheon, all heavy hitters of industry.

The first major victory for Bothwell and the National Committee for Responsive Philanthropy was obtaining participation of nontraditional charities in the Combined Federal Campaign. The Combined Federal Campaign is the largest workplace charity drive in the world. It is a federated fund-raising drive held in all U.S. government workplaces that had long been dominated by the United Way and traditional organizations like the Red Cross and the American Cancer Society.

The National Committee for Responsive Philanthropy also sponsored conferences to help racial and ethnic organizations learn how to pressure corporations to allow workplace-giving campaigns for all charities. They explained modern practices of fund-raising and publicity techniques. They also showed how to lead protest demonstrations. They received grants from major foundations, such as the Robert Wood Johnson Foundation, to conduct studies and publish pamphlets on corporate racial and ethnic community funding.

Over the years, they were able to develop respect and credibility. In the fall of 1999, for example, the director of Texaco's community relations and corporate giving programs flew to Washington to meet with the staff of the National Committee for Responsive Philanthropy to seek advice on how to be responsive to racial and ethnic minority agencies.

The ultimate success of Bothwell and his National Committee for Responsive Philanthropy is that the United Way no longer has monopoly rights in workplace giving. Employees are provided a choice in the annual community fund-raising drives. They can give to organizations supported by the United Way, selected United Way agencies, or any number of other community organizations by writing the name of the organization on the United Way pledge card. The United

Way honors the givers' request and administers the process of transferring the gift to the designated organizations.

Corporations can also designate all or part of the corporate donation in the same manner as employees do in the workplace campaign. A number of major companies now designate parts of their corporate gifts to charities other than just the United Way.

Donor choice, as it is called, is now commonplace in the annual United Way drive, so much so that it is estimated that, in some cities, close to 60 percent of the money raised by the United Way is designated for nonmember agencies of the United Way. The United Way, once a powerful fund-raising and community-planning agency, has become a contributions pass-through organization for community charities.

Confusion and concern is growing among corporate philanthropy officials as more and more organizations, inside and outside the United Way, compete directly for funds from their companies. It is a topic of concern at corporate citizenship workshops and conferences. A teleconference of 150 community relations managers conducted by The Center for Corporate Citizenship at Boston College on workplace giving, for example, was so popular that it had to be repeated three weeks later.

Since its victories in changing the fund-raising practices of the federal government agencies and the United Way, the National Committee for Responsive Philanthropy has become a watchdog organization challenging federal and state legislation that restricts racial and ethnic nonprofit fund-raising. It fought, for example, federal efforts to limit lobbying efforts of nonprofit organizations and attempts in some states to restrict the advocacy of nonprofit groups. It continues, it claims in its Web pages, to be an "aggressive defender of nonprofit rights."

PETA, PEOPLE FOR THE ETHICAL TREATMENT OF ANIMALS

At the 2003 national conference of the American Meat Institute Foundation, the keynote speaker stunned the audience that included representatives from major national chain restaurants, fast-food restaurants such as McDonald's, Burger King, KFC, Wendy's, and milk and animal producers by announcing, "The activists are beginning to win. And they know it."[6]

It was the last thing the audience wanted to hear, and, until 2000, was unimaginable. But beginning in the new century, a wide-ranging number of companies began shifting policies and practices to conform to the demands of animal rights activists.

In August 2000, for example, McDonald's notified its suppliers that they had to meet a set of minimum standards set by animal rights activists for treating hens. Florida amended its state constitution in 2002 to establish standards for confining pigs in sheds and cages. The major fast-food restaurants have hired "animal welfare specialists" to establish standards for the humane treatment of the animals that they would buy. The National Basketball Association switched from using balls made of cowhide to a synthetic product. And in June 2003, McDonald's told its suppliers not to use growth-promoting antibiotics that are fed to healthy animals.

Much of the success of these actions can be can be attributed to one organization—People for the Ethical Treatment of Animals, or PETA as it is most often called. Both admired and reviled, PETA is notoriously successful. It raises more than $15 million from some 750,000 members, many of them youngsters. Unlike other animal welfare organizations, such as the Society for the Prevention of Cruelty to Animals, PETA has been able to sensitize huge segments of the population to its attitudes on the treatment of animals.

But it is the way PETA has gone about implementing its mission that has both infuriated the public and made it successful. It attacked the fur industry by throwing paint and blood on celebrities in fur coats, paraded nude models on the streets of New York, publicized the treatment of animals used by fast-food restaurants in their food, allegedly sent threatening letters to pharmaceutical company scientists for using animals in drug experiments, compared the treatment of animals to the Nazi murder of six million Jews, and ran ads claiming beer was more nutritious than milk.

PETA claims to be an "abolitionist organization." Animals, according to PETA's mission statement, "are not to be used for food, clothing, entertainment, or experimentation. Animal rights means that animals, like humans, have interests that cannot be sacrificed or traded away just because it might benefit others."

Agree or disagree with the mission of the organization, few activist organizations can point to the success PETA has had in bringing about a seismic shift in corporate practices, not just in the United States but around the world. In a little more than twenty years, PETA has changed the way pharmaceutical companies treat animals in experimental laboratories; convinced millions of women, including celebrities, to give up wearing fur coats, causing millions of dollars in lost sales to the fur industry; and transformed the fast-food industry.

The founder, driving force, and single-minded leader of PETA is Ingrid Newkirk, who sees herself as part of a long history in liberating the weak and the unprotected—slaves, blacks, children, and women. Animals are just one more link in the chain of freeing a species of the universe, maintains Newkirk. While the organization has a board of directors, it is window dressing to preserve its nonprofit tax status. Newkirk is the organization.

Her belief in animal rights is unwavering. She is a vegetarian and does not use, wear, or eat animal products of any kind, including milk, eggs, and honey. And it is this belief that is the guiding principle of the organization.

She is PETA's creative force behind the shock and awe tactics of the organization. She recognizes that some tactics alienate members. Feminists hate the naked displays, she says, for example. But she sees herself and PETA as frontline shock troops in the relentless war against animal misuse and abuse. Animals have rights just as we do, she is reported to say, and that is why they should not be harmed, imposed upon, or used in any way. Easing the suffering of animals is a worthy objective, but it is never her goal, just a stop along the way.

She is, according to a profile article in the *New Yorker* magazine, moderating her views. She praises, for example, Burger King, an organizations she once picketed, for introducing a vegetarian sandwich. In 2003, she participated in Fashion Week instead of disrupting it.

When asked if she was softening her methods, she said, "You can't pave the road. You have to put down a little gravel. Then somebody else comes and puts down some more gravel. And one day, someday, you have a paved road."[7]

SUMMARY: THE LESSONS FROM THE FACES OF ACTIVISM

What do these vignettes tell us? First, most activists are not kooks, antibusiness zealots, or publicity hungry egotists. Except for a small few, they are sincerely and genuinely interested in the cause they are espousing. Some may be more passionate and strident in their behavior than others in advancing their cause, but that does not mean that they are any less genuine or sincere.

Second, activists come from all backgrounds, races, and strata in societies. They may be a neighbor protesting the expansion of a roadway needed for the operation of a company, a colleague volunteering for an organization that wants to expand women's rights, the son or daughter of a colleague who is organizing boycotts against companies that have unsafe labor practices in developing countries, or the aunt or uncle organizing their friends, families, and neighbors to support the Kyoto Protocol. They are the faces of people everywhere in the new activist world.

Third, no one is without the potential power, whether it be a prince, a retired social worker, or a storekeeper in Ugborodo, Nigeria, to affect the actions of a company through influencing legislation, regulations, or public and community opinion.

Fourth, all NGOs are advocates for a cause, regardless of their primary mission. As I pointed out earlier, The American Cancer Society is a powerful antismoking organization that has caused cigarette smoking to decrease. The American Lung Association is an activist for improving clean air legislation, claiming that the increase in asthma and other respiratory illnesses can be directly linked to truck and automobile pollution. It has begun a campaign to demand that the government place the interests of the American public above political and business interests.[8]

Fifth, activist organizations, such as Greenpeace, the Committee for Responsive Philanthropy, or PETA, engage in what community planners call "opportunistic decision making." They seek out projects that can create favorable publicity for the organization to bolster their fundraising and membership recruiting programs. Greenpeace's efforts to halt Shell from disposing of a used oil rig in the north Atlantic Ocean is a classic example.

Sixth, while it is far from common, the temptation for advocacy organizations to slant the news, embellish pronouncements, or even falsify information is great. Greenpeace, for example, based its campaign on the environmental damage that would be created from the leaking of millions of gallons of oil from Shell's Brent Spar oil rig. In truth, there was very little oil that would be leaked, a point that Greenpeace staff later admitted they knew and for which they apologized in their annual report.

Seventh, advocacy organizations tend to moderate their tactics over time. Called the regression to the mean effect, PETA's efforts to soften its actions, described earlier, is one example.

Another, for example, is the change in tactics from militancy to collaboration and cooperation by the AIDS organization, Act Up. Founded in 1987 as an advocacy and social change organization, it used militant tactics to pressure the federal government and the health professions to increase research and treatment for AIDS victims. Act Up gained worldwide attention by disrupting government meetings and halting, briefly, trading on the New York Stock Exchange. Ten years later, the *New York Times*, in a feature article titled "At 10, Act Up Doesn't Much, Anymore," reported that Act Up's activism has matured. It has changed, according to the *Times*, "from attention-getting temper tantrums to a more seasoned, reasoned perspective."[9]

Regression to the mean is a product of success. The more successful an advocacy organization becomes in its fund-raising and membership drives, the more it is forced to modify its views and actions to accommodate the views and opinions of new members. It also is a function of the loss of enthusiasm. Succeeding generations of followers lack the unbridled energy and crisis mentality of the founders.

Eighth, and most important, activists and activist groups are successful because of the connections they develop and maintain. It does not take many people to initiate a trend or an action. But it does take people who have a network of connections that they maintain by their social skills. They are known as social connectors.[10]

Mama Ayo, the shop keeper in Ugborodo, Nigeria, is a classic example of a social connector. She sits in front of her store greeting passersby and chatting with customers. She is inquisitive. She is interested in her village and the people in the village. She is persuasive. There is little in the village that Mama Ayo does not know, the very characteristics of a social connector.

CHAPTER 4

Step One: You Start with a Vision— A Social Vision

In the early 1980s, a number of companies began to realize that they needed a vision to give some direction to the planning of community relations programs. Aware that companies used a business vision to design their business strategies and goals, they felt that a similar vision was needed to guide the development of community strategies.

Some used the term *social* vision to define the kind of vision that could be used to define community relations strategies.[1] Others, uncomfortable with the word *social,* used the term *community*. Regardless of what was used, there was a significant realization that defining some kind of vision was needed for planning community programs. Consequently, a majority of companies began developing social or community visions for planning purposes.

With the advent of corporate citizenship in the late 1990s and early 2000s, there was a growing recognition that the earlier social or community vision was too limiting. Corporate citizenship encompasses a much broader array of activities, including the environment, ethics, transparency, human rights, child labor, and diversity as well as community involvement. A newer vision was needed to guide the development of a company's citizenship strategies.

Fewer companies, moreover, were now not uncomfortable with the term *social* vision. After all, the company's citizenship programs were responses to social issues. Moreover, people began using the term *social visionary* to describe CEOs who were in the forefront of corporate citizenship.

The new social vision was not distinct from nor the same as a business vision. A business vision includes statements of why the company exists, what purpose it serves, and how the company should be positioned in the future. It provides direction, drives change, motivates and energizes employees, gives context to strategies, and influences mangers in their decision making. It is also a public statement, a signal to shareholders, analysts, and business leaders that describes the prospects for growth and the vitality of the company.

But a business vision alone is no longer sufficient for success in the activist society. Needed also is a social vision, a statement of the company's core operating values and the benefits it wants to make to society as it goes about carrying out its business goals and objectives. The social vision guides the collective behavior of the company and gives direction to how the company should act in its relationships with external stakeholders.

WHY THE NEED FOR A SOCIAL VISION?

A prime reason for a social vision is that it reassures stakeholders that the company intends to adhere to the new rules of corporate behavior—safeguard the environment; support human rights; eliminate child labor; adopt codes of ethics; enter into partnerships with nongovernmental organizations; display openness and transparency in relationships with customers, employees, community groups, and governmental organizations; promote diversity in the workplace; help communities solve their social problems; support local, national, and international charities; and pay their fair share of taxes.

A second reason is that it is plain old good business. Studies by The Center for Corporate Citizenship at Boston College, and others, reveal that shareholders, employees, customers, government officials, activists, and the public have overwhelmingly favorable attitudes toward companies that demonstrate they are responsive to the quality of life issues in communities and societies.[2] And when customers, employees, and key public officials know a company has adopted and lives up to a social vision, the favorable attitudes increase. A social vision also makes it easier to establish relationships with key officials, and the relationships tend to be more loyal and trusting, according to the studies.[3]

Third, a social vision is a distinguishing mark of a world-class company. Admired companies, companies that have the respect and trust of their peers, customers, and employees, have a vision that is broader than their economic or business vision. Merck, the widely admired pharmaceutical company, continues to quote the words of its founder

George W. Merck to guide its business strategies: "We try never to forget that medicine is for people. Not for profits. The profits will follow, and if we have remembered that, they have never failed to appear."

While world-class companies are proud of their products and services, revel in creativity and innovation, and are continually attentive to the needs of customers and clients. World-class companies are continually attentive to the changing social, environmental, and ethical needs and attitudes of the public. Responding to the accounting and governance scandal of the 2002s, for example, the Coca-Cola Company changed its accounting practices to report the value of stock options it granted to executives as an expense. This was a daring move, challenging the common wisdom of most corporations. But it had to be done, according to Coke's CEO, Douglas N. Daft, to get ahead of a growing distrust and anger against corporations that were making their presence felt by a precipitous drop in the stock markets. "We know," explained Coke's chief financial officer, "we're in a new environment and we need to take the lead on this issue and perhaps in a small way, try to help restore confidence in corporate America."[4] Other companies quickly followed Coke's lead.

World-class companies, moreover, see no incompatibility between a business vision and a social vision. Indeed, a social vision is viewed as an integral part of a world-class company's business vision. "We do not see our social responsibilities," says Sir Peter Middleton, chairman of Barclays Bank, "as conflicting with business objectives, neither do we see them as add-on. Providing progressive employment practices and excellent customer service, minimising our impact on the environment and supporting the wider community all help to define who we are and how we differ from our competitors. We see our role as a good corporate citizen as helping to build a stronger business."

THE CHARACTERISTICS OF A SOCIAL VISION

A social vision is a statement about the company's social, environmental, and ethical obligations to communities and societies. It is designed to give direction and focus to the way a company will act in society as it goes about achieving its business goals and strategies. It is a pledge to internal and external stakeholders that the company will operate in ways that

- contribute to the development of communities in which it operates;
- respond sensitively to the concerns and issues of communities and societies;
- maintain and sustain the environment for present and future generations;
- treat its employees with dignity and respect;
- foster human rights;
- engage in ethical and open relationships with shareholders, employees, customers, and community officials; and
- work collaboratively with external stakeholders in addressing community and societal concerns and issues.

It is recognition, too, that social, environmental, and ethical issues and concerns have a direct relationship to the company's ability to be successful. It answers the following questions: What do we want the public to say about the behavior of this company? How do we want to behave as we go about operating in communities and societies? What values do we want to add to the communities in which we operate? What environmental legacy do we want to hand down to our successors?

While the vision grows out of assessments of changing trends, attitudes, issues, and concerns of external stakeholders, it is first and foremost a statement by the company. It is a pledge that the company—not a stakeholder—makes to confirm the integrity of the company's behavior.

Equally important, it is a product of an *objective* analysis of public social, environmental, and ethical trends and issues. It is a factual assessment. Objectivity is important if only to avoid the easy temptation to blame or to question the sincerity of outsiders for the problems a company may face in communities and societies. Faulting activists or the government winds up in a search for excuses not solutions to the problems many companies face in their relationships in communities and societies.

The CEO is the driving force for developing and managing the social vision. Similar to the business vision, the social vision must be the creation of the chief executive officer. In fact, according to a survey of 1,500 senior leaders, 870 of whom were CEOs, designing a vision is the principal behavior trait desired in a CEO. The job of the CEO, according to the respondents, is to convey "a strong sense of vision."[5]

The CEO not only has to be the molder of the vision but also its champion. The days when the CEO was the civic cheerleader in the community are over. Mergers and acquisitions as a consequence of globalization are shrinking the number of CEOs, and those who are left have little time for heading up a museum gala or a community development effort. What precious free time a CEO has is now expected to be spent with the family.

The new "civic" job of the CEO is to promote the social vision inside the company and to ensure that it is being carried out. If the social vision is to be an enduring guide to management decision–making, then it is the CEO who must ask the questions: Does this business decision support the kind of company we want to be in society? Does it detract from the social vision of our company?

Another reason why CEOs have to be responsible for shaping and managing the social vision is their new "celebrity" role. Today's CEOs are recognized and sought after for opinions. They appear on business television channels and talk shows, make speeches at public forums, and write best-selling books. They are questioned not just about the economic performance of their own companies but about business in general.

And they are also asked questions about social and environmental responsibility, including their own company's responsibility to society. When the answers do not conform to the public's new rules for corporate behavior, they are faulted. Jack Welch, for example, has seen his legacy as the most admired CEO in the country become tarnished because of the way he fought against removing a toxic chemical, polychlorinated biphenyls (PCB), the company had dumped into the Hudson River. "There are many, even in corporate America," wrote Joseph Nocera, executive editor of *Fortune* magazine, "who believe that the ferocity with which G.E. fought to avoid having to clean up the river was the single biggest mistake of the Welch era."[6]

Writing in the *Harvard Business Review*, Warren Bennis, the Distinguished Professor of Business Administration at the University of Southern California, referred to the PCB issue as one of the two famous failures of Welch's tenure. The other was the aborted Honeywell acquisition, which itself is an example of Welch's refusal to understand that the rules for corporate behavior had changed.[7] Ironically, Welch's predecessor, Reginald Jones, is quoted by the Business Roundtable, an organization of the chief executive officers of major companies, as saying, "public policy and social issues are no longer adjuncts to business planning and management. They are in the mainstream of it. The concern must be pervasive in companies today, from boardroom to factory floor."[8]

Corporate social issues have now become a form of public account-ability. And if the CEO is to be held publicly accountable for the company's social and environmental performance, then it behooves the CEO to take responsibility for shaping and managing its social vision.

A social vision needs to be explicit—repeatedly explicit. Managers should not have to guess how the company expects them to behave in their relationships with external stakeholders. It should be as in-delible in their minds as the company's business vision. It has to be intrinsic to the culture of the organization—the "this is the way we do things here" expression of the behavior of the people who work for the company.

On an accompanying page are sample vision statements. Some are simple and forthright. Others emphasize relationships with commu-nities. Still others, more modern social visions, highlight the obliga-tions to employees, customers, the environment, and the economic stability of communities—increasingly becoming called "the triple bottom line." See Table 4.1 for sample vision statements.

A common characteristic of these vision statements is their simplic-ity, conciseness, and clarity. Business visions are rarely long-winded. Jack Welch's famous and successful business vision for G.E., soon after becoming CEO in 1980, is a good example: It is necessary, he told his managers, for G.E. to become "number one or two in every thing we do—or do something about it."[9] Nothing could be clearer. And it certainly worked.

A social vision, like a business vision, should not be a "white" paper or a complicated description of the company's social programs. It should be a straightforward explanation of how the company wants to be perceived by employees, customers, shareholders, vendors, com-munity stakeholders, and the general public.

Repeatedly explicit means that the social vision should be promoted whenever possible. Jack Welch, for example, kept hammering on his business vision at any occasion. "Like every goal and initiative we've ever launched, I repeated the No. 1 or No. 2 message over and over again until I nearly gagged," said Welch. "I tried to sell both the in-tellectual and emotional cases for doing it. The organization had to see every management action aligned with the vision."[10]

Because it is a societal vision, it should be made publicly explicit. Why hide a concept that influences customers, employees, and pub-lic officials? State it. Publicize it. Promote it in all sorts of ways.

Significantly, there is a growing movement to publish profession-ally attractive corporate social or social responsibility annual reports.

Table 4.1
Sample Vision Statements

McDonald's

We are committed
To doing what is right,
To being a good neighbor and partner in the community,
To conduct our business with the environment in mind.

Michigan Automotive Compressor (MACI)

"MACI clearly recognizes a responsibility to fulfill the duties and obligations of a local community member.

We welcome this challenge and opportunity, and we affirm our belief that investment in our community is a wise investment in our well-being.

We understand that our success is directly related to the quality of life enjoyed by our associates and families, and to the economic and social well-being of our community."

BC Hydro

Our mission is to provide integrated energy solutions to our customers in an environmentally and socially responsible manner. In other words, to provide power in a way that is sustainable in the long term. We believe it is essential not only to make a profit, but also to care about people and protect the environment—and to be accountable for all three. We call it our "Triple Bottom Line."

Royal Dutch Shell

We are striving to fulfill our commitments to society, based on our strong Business Principles. This includes using the principles of sustainable development in all our operations—taking account of their social and environmental consequences as well as the economic dimension. We believe long-term competitive success depends on being trusted to meet society's expectations.

Johnson & Johnson

We are responsible to the communities in which we live and work and to the world community as well. We must be good citizens—support good works and charities and bear our fair share of taxes. We must encourage civic improvements and better health and education. We must maintain in good order the property we are privileged to use, protecting the environment and natural resources.

Ford Motor Company

"A good company delivers excellent products and services, a great one delivers excellent products and services and strives to make the world a better place." (William Clay Ford, Chairman and CEO)

The old low-cost community relations report has taken on a new luster. It has also attracted attention. Ford's first annual social report, *Connecting with Society*, earned it a front-page story in the *New York Times* and was also praised in an editorial a few days later.[11]

Consistency is equally as important as explicitness. A vision statement is long-range in scope. It gives direction to strategic planning and provides a framework for day-to-day decision making. Unlike goals and objectives, it should not fluctuate or be subject to individual whims. It explains what the organization will do when confronted by ambiguity and surprises.[12] Changing a company's social vision should be done cautiously and thoughtfully. The consequence of inconsistency can be disastrous.

When Monsanto, for example, was preparing to implement its biotechnology strategy in the late 1980s, it was well aware of the fears and uncertainty of the public toward bioengineered food products. It knew, too, that there was strong organized opposition among many environmental groups to bioengineering. A strategy committee was charged with gaining public acceptance of the company's push into biotechnology. One of the original strategies was to bring in opponents as consultants, believing that their involvement in the process would ease bioengineered food into the marketplace. Plans were developed to reach out to affected groups, environmentalists, farmers, agricultural universities, food companies, and public officials in hopes of winning their support. This approach would be time consuming—probably ten years long, according to Monsanto's chief operating officer at the time.

In the late 1980s, however, to the great surprise of the strategy committee, the company, dissatisfied with the go-slow approach, suddenly reversed course and adopted a government affairs strategy at the direction of the newly appointed CEO, Robert Shapiro, whose background was urban policy. A new management team experienced in government affairs took over the biotechnology planning. The go-slow approach was shelved in favor of a strategy that would tackle the regulatory barriers head-on. Government guidelines would speed up public acceptance. They hastily began meeting with elected and appointed government officials in Washington.

The original committee members argued against tampering with collaboration and consultation, a strategic approach that had worked well for the company in the past. Caution, they insisted, should by the byword of the biotechnology strategy. The new managers hurried on, however. Without any advanced warning to the public and against the advice of scientists, they began introducing biotechnology products. Bovine growth hormone, which improves milk production, was quickly introduced, followed by bioengineered bacteria designed to make plants resistant to frost. Newspapers printed photographs of scientists in protective gear, including respirators, spraying strawberry plants. The public was horrified. Environmental opponents were delighted.

The strategy blew up in Monsanto's face. Public furor was unrelenting, and resistance to biotechnology spread and intensified. By the end of the 1980s, Monsanto's error in abandoning its slow collaborative strategy was apparent. "I don't think they really thought through the whole darn thing," said a professor of biological sciences at Stanford University.[13]

Shapiro admitted failure. "We've learned that there is a fine line between scientific excitement on the one hand and corporate arrogance on the other," he wrote. "We've been working with biotechnology for twenty years. We think we know something about the subject, perhaps more than most people. When we think that about ourselves, it's not hard to give people the impression that we don't much care what they think—that our job is to teach (or preach) and theirs to listen respectfully. We didn't listen very well to people who insisted there were relevant ethical, religious, cultural, social, and economic issues as well."[14]

Ironically, Monsanto had at that time, and still does have, strong, positive, and supportive relationships in its manufacturing communities. The support and positive reputation of the company is based on an implicit vision that its community and environmental programs and strategies should support the goal of enhancing and protecting the company's license to operate. To a person, Monsanto managers will tell you that, in today's cynical and litigious world, obtaining the permission to operate is essential in running a facility. Maintaining that permission, they maintain, requires developing positive, sustainable, and collaborative relationships with individuals, organizations, and groups in communities—which seems like the beginning of an effective social vision.

A social vision should be global in scope. Community relations practices are much more mature than they were just ten years ago. They are more strategic, better managed, more successful, and a good deal more professionally operated. Consequently, managers have benefited from a rich experience in designing long-range "community" and "social" visions on how to position a company favorably in a community.

The success of community relations, however, has led to a tendency in companies to neglect the development of a global social vision, believing that a vision that works at the community level is sufficient to guide it in international operations. The problem with this reasoning, however, is that international issues can often be far different and often more complex than local issues. And when confronted by an international issue, corporate officers, many inexperienced in modern community affairs, fall back on practices that are based on the old rules of community relations.

The inability of major pharmaceutical companies to succeed in a lawsuit to prevent the South African government from purchasing generic AIDS drugs described earlier is one example. Leaders from around the world, including Nelson Mandela, former president of South Africa; Kofi Annan, Secretary General of the United Nations; and officials at Yale University where one of the AIDS drugs was developed, attempted to convince the drug companies that their objections were unrealistic. The drug companies persisted in their suit, despite evidence that the litigation tactic was failing. On April 19, 2001, two years after the suit was filed, the pharmaceutical companies finally relented.

The ironic lesson is that, at the community level, pharmaceutical companies had long foresworn litigation as a tactic in dealing with community groups and activists. They had been building, quite successfully, strategies based on a vision that consultation and collaboration should be the guiding force of programs and in working with community groups. This experience could have been an informed source for a company-wide social vision and may well have averted the failure in South Africa.

A social vision should be individually tailored to a company. There may be similarities in practices and programs, but each company must develop its own vision and methods for achieving it. A social vision, for example, for a high-technology company may be different from that of a chemical manufacturing company. They each respond to different societal concerns and issues. Public utilities often have to emphasize the importance of responding to community concerns that large global manufacturing companies may not. Societal and community issues are different in California from those in New England. What is an important concern in the Philippines may not be the same in the United Kingdom.

The social vision should also relate to the unique values and competencies of a company. Almost every company has something that is distinctive—the product or service the company offers; the values of its founders and current leaders; the special culture, knowledge, creativity, and expertise of its employees; and the vision the company has as a business. Capturing this distinctiveness in a social vision statement can be a powerful force for integrating its acceptance and adherence throughout the company.

Excerpts from Johnson & Johnson's Credo, elsewhere in this document, present a good example of how a pharmaceutical company emphasizes one of its distinctive characteristics—health—in a social vision.

A social vision is a management responsibility. Finally and probably the most difficult requirement to implement is to make corporate citizenship a responsibility of senior officers and managers in a company. All too often, general managers assume that corporate citizenship is an enhanced or expanded community relations function. Nothing could be further from the truth. General managers are the visible presence of the company in the community and in society. They set the tone. They determine the actions of the company. Consequently, communities look to the manager, not the public relations or public affairs official, to explain the company's behavior.

That means using the social vision as a guide to individual behavior and decision making. As Susan Rice, CEO of Lloyds Bank of Scotland, explained at a Center for Corporate Citizenship at Boston College annual conference, "Corporate citizenship is best practiced when it is integrated in the company. Business decisions need to be made against the background of their impact on community and society. And corporate citizenship decisions should be made against the background of business needs."

Of course, getting general managers to accept the operational responsibility of a social vision is a monumental task. It requires a shift in culture, a transformation on how the company is operated and run. No change of this magnitude is ever easy. It means giving up old habits and relationships. It means learning new ways to relate to a much wider group of stakeholders than is customary now. But the adoption and implementation of a social vision is no longer optional for today's managers. It is mandatory in the activist society.

How this can be accomplished is described in the next few chapters.

CHAPTER 5

Step Two: Abandon the Command and Control Style of Managing External Affairs

Ask managers, "Do you need community buy-in for your company and its operations?" Inevitably, the answer is, "Yes." Ask why, and they will say, "It's a license-to-operate issue. You need the permission of the community to operate."

If there is such widespread agreement that companies need community permission to operate, why, then, do so many consistently run into protests and opposition to their plans, intentions, and operations? Why do they antagonize the public and, very often, alienate their staunchest supporters?

There are two reasons. One, they rely on a style of relationships with external stakeholders that no longer work. And, second, they do not have a plan to obtain community buy-in.

We begin with two examples—not the exceptions but, all too often, the rule.

THE WALT DISNEY COMPANY AND ITS HISTORY THEME PARK

In early 1991, The Walt Disney Company began exploring the Washington, D.C., area to achieve a long-sought dream of the company's president and CEO, Michael Eisner—build a history theme park. It was Eisner's contention, and one supported by surveys and studies conducted by education organizations, that American youngsters were hugely ignorant of their country's history. We can change this, thought Eisner, by using the Disney creative skills and talents to make history informative and entertaining.[1]

Of course, not lost on the Disney executives was that the nation's capital was a prime tourist attraction. Close to 20 million people visit Washington annually. It looked like a brilliant business decision and win-win idea for the company and the nation.

In 1993, they settled on a 3,000 acre site in Haymarket, Virginia, less than twenty miles from the capital. Close to 2,300 acres was owned by Exxon. When questions of possible community objections were raised, they were quickly dismissed "[S]ince the site," explained the team, "had already been zoned once for a large, residential and commercial development, we wouldn't have a problem—and indeed the local residents would welcome thousands of jobs in an area that was struggling economically."

Furthermore, the development team believed that persuading the Virginia legislature to underwrite infrastructure improvements—widening the interstate, building access roads, and utilities—would be easy. After all, the project would create new jobs, generate additional tax revenues, and attract tourists flush with money to spend in Virginia communities.

Secretly and quietly, the company began buying up the land. Even Exxon was unaware that Disney was the buyer of their parcel.

But keeping it secret was becoming difficult. And even before the company could notify local and state officials, including the newly elected governor, George Allen, news of the impending park began to leak out. The *Washington Post* broke the story on the front page of the Metropolitan section on November 10, 1993, under the foreboding headline: "In Disney's Grand Plan, Some See a Smoggy Cloggy Transportation Mess."

Within five days of the *Post* story, the opposition became galvanized. Led by the National Trust for Historical Preservation, a committee called Protect Historic America was quickly formed and headed up by Richard Moe, a former White House official in the Carter administration. It included some of America's most noted historians: David McCullough, Ken Burns, C. Vann Woodward, John Hope Franklin, and Roger Wilkins, to name a few. Claiming that the Disney Company would trivialize American history and destroy the nearby Manassas Civil War battleground, they were able to recruit 200 historians from across the country to their cause. Included also in the opposition were some very wealthy residents whose estates were located west of the proposed theme park—the Grahams (owners of the *Washington Post*) the Mellons, the DuPonts, and the Harrimans.

But the company successfully recruited the support of community officials and local residents of Haymarket. They also secured the backing of Governor Allen; the previous governor, Douglas Wilder; key state legislators; and local community officials, including the powerful chairwoman of the county Board of Supervisors. They were also able to obtain key zoning changes and environmental approvals in the summer of 1994.

They persuaded the state legislature to approve a $140 million bond offering for highway improvements and another $20 million to support a marketing campaign for Virginia historical points, including the Disney theme park. The Disney people were optimistic and enthusiastic at these initial successes.

Nonetheless, opposition to the project continued to grow. National leaders began to weigh in, including federal officials. The Secretary of the Interior, Bruce Babbit, for example, announced he was considering an investigation.

Disney countered with a publicity drive. The Disney people announced that the project would generate 12,000 new jobs, 1.86 billion dollars of tax revenues, and thousands of dollars annually in donations to local charities. The park would be a windfall for northern Virginia.

In early June 1994, Eisner met with editors of the *Washington Post*—the most vigorous and public opponent of the project. Eisner felt that the *Post* had been too harsh and one-sided in its commentaries and news stories, and he wanted an opportunity to present his side of the benefits of the theme park to the community.

But it backfired. News reports of the meeting in the *Post* on June 14 described Eisner as defensive and angry. He was quoted as saying, "I'm shocked, because I thought we were doing good." To add insult to injury, Eisner criticized the historians. "I sat through many history classes where I read some of their stuff, and I didn't learn anything. It was pretty boring."

Eisner's reactions only added fuel for the opposition. It attracted more supporters, including such political luminaries as John Kenneth Galbraith, Bill Moyers, George Will, and Mary Matalin. The Disney venture became national news. The *New York Times*, in an editorial on June 19, told the company to abandon its theme park plans.

Once again, Eisner resorted to a media pitch. He answered with a letter to the *Times* published on June 23. The company, he explained, was not going to build on a Civil War battlefield. It was not going to

detract from history. It was not going to add to environmental concerns. "We plan," promised Eisner, "to comply with every regulatory
requirement and build a park that will do something that has never
been done in quite this way before. Using all the tools available to
us—film making, animation, music, interactive media, and live inter-
pretation—we will bring our American experience to life. We may thus
stir our young people to learn more about our country."[2]

But it was too late. Delays, legal fights, and lobbying costs were
threatening the future profitability of the project. It was becoming too
costly.

Eisner wanted to continue. After all, the park represented only $650
million in a company worth $22 billion. Nonetheless, the opposition
was wearing the company down. "[It] looked like it was going to drag
on and on, and it just wasn't worth the abuse. It wasn't fun anymore,"
one Disney official was quoted in the *Wall Street Journal*.[3]

On Wednesday, September 29, 1994, Eisner relented and announced that the company was giving up on its plans to build a theme
park in Haymarket, Virginia. The opposition rejoiced and celebrated.
"Historians, writers and ordinary citizens won a victory for the national heritage," wrote the *New York Times* on September 30, 1994,
in an editorial headlined "Disney Retreats at Bull Run." "The Walt
Disney Company abandoned the most irresponsible idea ever hatched
in the Magic Kingdom and decided not to build a theme park near
Manassas Battlefield in Prince William County, Virginia."[4]

THE GENERAL ELECTRIC COMPANY'S
POLLUTION BATTLES IN MASSACHUSETTS
AND NEW YORK

On August 1, 2001, Christie Whitman, the then administrator of
the Environmental Protection Agency, announced she was upholding
an order issued by democratic President William Clinton in the last
days of his presidency that would require the General Electric Company to dredge and remove a suspected cancer-causing chemical, polychlorinated biphenyls (PCBs), from the Hudson River. G.E. officials
were shocked and furious, particularly Jack Welch, the CEO. He had
depended on the newly elected George W. Bush Republican administration to overturn Clinton's directive. After all, Whitman began her
tenure by turning back all of the Clinton last-minute environmental
directives, including one aimed at reducing the level of arsenic in drinking water that created a huge outcry. (She later reversed her suspen-

sion of the Clinton arsenic standard, and less than a year after she re-signed, the arsenic decision was reversed again.) On top of all that Welch was a personal friend of President Bush and a major backer in his campaign for president.

PCB is a liquid chemical used as an insulating fluid to reduce the risk of fires in electrical products. G.E. used PCBs in the manufacture of metal housings of transformers and capacitors as early as the mid 1940s. Waste containing the chemical was discharged into New York's Hudson River and Massachusetts's Housatonic River in Springfield.

In the late 1960s and early 1970s, disturbing studies conducted by New York State officials and publicized by *Sports Illustrated* revealed that high levels of PCBs were found in fish flesh and eggs caught in the Hudson River. Studies with animals revealed a link between PCB and cancer. Later studies—disputed, incidentally, by G.E.—revealed that PCB also caused cancer in humans. Researchers were finding disturbing effects of PCB on expectant mothers. One, reported in the *New England Journal of Medicine*, found that children born of mothers who had eaten fish containing PCB had IQ deficits, poor reading comprehension, memory problems, and attention deficits.[5]

G.E. chemists were also encountering disturbing stories about the high rate of cancer in employees working with PCBs. G.E. did not immediately reveal the results of its studies on the dangers of PCB to its own employees, many of whom later died of cancer said to be a direct result of working with PCBs.[6] Jack Welch, former CEO of G.E., denies the validity of these studies.[7]

G.E. contends that it dumped PCBs into the rivers when it was not an illegal substance, which is true. It further claims that the order to dredge the Hudson River at a cost likely to exceed a half a billion dollars is based on spurious science and may indeed make matters worse. It would cause a resuspension of buried PCBs, tear up the river banks, knock trees down to widen the roads, and destroy the ecosystem. It would be an environmental disaster, according to Welch.[8]

Whitman's decision ended a twenty-five-year-long dispute with G.E. when former CEO Jack Welch first learned at a meeting in 1977 that government officials were likely to demand that G.E. remove PCBs from the Housatonic and Hudson Rivers and from yards of residents of Pittsfield, Massachusetts, where PCB-laden soil was dumped. It involved not just the EPA but governors of two states (Pataki of New York and Celluci of Massachusetts), environmental organizations, community residents, and former G.E. employees.

G.E. depended on a number of tactics and strategies to respond to the PCB issue. One was stall and delay to frustrate complainants. When, for example, a Pittsfield resident discovered that land beneath his business was contaminated with PCBs, he asked G.E. to buy the property or clean it up. It took years to negotiate with the company and no terms were ever agreed upon. By the time the resident tried to sue the company, the statute of limitations had run out. G.E. willingly admits using the statute of limitations as a defense tactic.[9]

It used a similar tactic to keep company-sponsored research on the health consequences of PCB on humans from the public. In 1981, for example, G.E. recruited a Harvard University researcher, David Wegman, to conduct a study of worker mortality among former employees of its Pittsfield plant. The workers claimed that there were significantly high deaths from leukemia and intestinal cancer as a result of working with PCBs. Wegman's study was completed in March 1983. The company announced it would release Wegman's findings in three months. Years passed and the study results failed to materialize. When former employees asked for the Wegman study results, they were met repeatedly with resistance. "As much as you hate to say it," claimed on of the employees, "I think the stonewalling was deliberate."[10]

The company spent an estimated $60 million on a publicity program to tell its story. It printed brochures, made speeches, sent out news releases, and published a newsletter called *River Watch: A Report on the EPA's Reassessment of the Hudson River.*[11] The EPA forced G.E. to change the title of the newsletter because it gave the impression it was government authored and sanctioned. It lobbied Congress to insert a rider in the 2000 environmental legislation that would exempt its responsibility to clean up the Hudson River. After protests, the rider was removed. It threatened to close its highly successful plastic plant in Pittsfield because residents were seeking to make the land where the PCBs were buried a superfund site, which could have made the company responsible for triple the costs of the cleanup.[12]

Probably its most reprehensible tactic was labeled by G.E. officials as "The Book-of-the-Month Club" strategy. Using the Freedom of Information Act, the company flooded government agencies with requests for information while continuing to delay government actions to make the company comply with federal directives. "If you don't hear from us, we assume you agree with us," is the gist of the strategy.

It was developed by Stephan D. Ramsey, vice president for Environmental Affairs, who was once employed by the environmental enforcement agency of the federal Department of Justice. He later joined the prestigious law firm Sidley and Austin where he authored a manual, based on his experience with the Justice Department, on how to stymie the government in pursuing environmental claims.[13]

Ramsey made extensive use of the Book-of-the-Month-Club strategy in G.E.'s battles with state and federal agencies. An angry regional administrator of the Environmental Protection Agency commented, "I don't like having our resources tied up this way. . . . I find many of their efforts objectionable in the extreme." Asked if they thought any of the requests were frivolous, a lawyer assigned to the case responded, "I guess frivolous is not the word I would use. I'd call them harassing."[14]

These tactics and strategies may have bought G.E. time, and it may have saved the company money in claims costs, but in the final analysis, the company was forced to comply with federal rules. Governor Pataki of New York, environmental activists, and the great majority of community residents along the Hudson River hailed administrator Whitman's decision. In an editorial, the *New York Times* stated, "Environmentalists who have regularly been disappointed by the performance and policies of the Bush administration got something big to cheer about on Tuesday. It came in the form of a difficult and admirable decision by Christie Whitman, the administrator."[15]

Welch called it the most frustrating issue he had to deal with in his twenty-five-year career at G.E.[16]

THE DAD STRATEGY

The Disney and G.E. disputes are examples of the Decide-Announce-Defend (DAD)[17] strategy for responding to public and community opposition. Most companies, like Disney, fall back on a DAD strategy, often unthinkingly, when they are taken by surprise. "I expected to be carried around on people's shoulders," said Eisner. Instead, he and the Disney planning team found themselves continuously defending what they assumed would be a welcome theme park.

A few, like G.E., use DAD consciously and deliberately as a planning strategy. When Welch, for example, first heard about accusations in 1975 that G.E. was going to be held responsible for cleaning up the PCBs it had dumped in the Hudson River, he reportedly told his executives, "On this one guys, let's just keep two steps ahead of the law."[18]

There are several problems with the DAD strategy. First, it is based on the assumption that there is only one solution to a problem. The company is right and the activists are wrong. As a consequence, people take sides, and the search for solutions becomes contaminated in stubbornness. Blame is often claimed to be poor communication. "We had lost the perception game," said Eisner. "Largely through our own missteps the Walt Disney Company had been effectively portrayed as an enemy of American history and a plunderer of sacred ground."

Second, the issue and the process become personalized. Outsiders get blamed. "It's about politics and punishing a successful company," claimed Jack Welch. "It's really a case where good science and common sense have become drowned out by loud voices and extreme views—to prod the government to punish a large global corporation. When they [corporations] are big they're an easy target," Welch added. "And when they are winners, they're an even bigger target."[19]

Third, without a plan, managers are constantly reacting to accusations and complaints. They become frustrated and angry. Eisner admitted he alienated the *Washington Post*'s editorial board at the June 14 meeting. "I was flip and defiant. My comments made me sound not just smug and arrogant but like something of a Philistine. Looking back, I realize how much my brief moment of intemperance undermined our cause."

Welch blew it with anger. One widely reported incident was a shouting match Welch had with a nun during the company's shareholder meeting in April 1998 when she announced that the company's claims that PCBs were harmless were no different than the claims made by the tobacco industry about the harmlessness of smoking.

"That's an outrageous comparison," Welch shouted at the nun. "You owe it to God to be on the side of truth."

"He totally lost it," said Sister Pat, a Dominican nun from New Jersey.[20]

Fourth, the strategy treats the issue not the outrage. The public resorts to activist action when it is outraged and angry. It has nothing to do with the issue itself. In South Boston, Massachusetts, as I mentioned earlier, a group of working-class neighbors became outraged when they learned that a football stadium for the professional New England Patriots team was planned for their community. They believed that the stadium would disrupt the community and create traffic problems.

The Patriots' management responded by pointing out the benefits of the stadium to Massachusetts. They then sought the approval of city and state officials, including the governor and mayor, and mounted a high-powered public relations campaign. These tactics were aimed at developing pressure from football fans, public officials, and even the Cardinal and, thus, win over the neighbors.

They never dealt with the neighbors' concerns and the reason for the outrage, and, therefore, lost the issue. As crisis communication expert, Peter Sandman points out that to avoid a crisis, first deal with the reasons for the outrage.[21] Ironically, a large convention center has been built in the location once planned for the stadium.

Fifth, the strategy alienates potential supporters. Two republican governors, Pataki in New York and Celluci in Massachusetts, were forced to side with the environmentalists because of the stall, delay, and litigation tactics of G.E. Each governor could have been a powerful ally in G.E.'s cause with environmentalists and community activists if each had been listened to at the earliest beginnings of the disputes.

Sixth, the basic failure of the DAD strategy is that it is based on a style of management that no longer works: command and control, a style of management that was abandoned by companies in its relationship with employees when it began to fail to work precisely for the very same reasons companies are now finding it isn't working in relationships with communities and societies.

The questionable efficacy of command and control management started in the 1960s and 1970s. Rising incomes along with better education were changing employee motivations. Comfortable with their material status, or subsistence-level needs, employees, particularly the managerial level of employees, were looking to satisfy social and egoistic needs, a set of needs higher in the hierarchy of needs. They were interested in growing professionally and personally. Under these changed conditions, the carrot and stick theory of supervision was found wanting.[22]

Motivations underlying the expectations the public has for corporations have also been changing. Traditionally, communities have been satisfied with the material benefits companies provided to their communities: jobs, tax benefits, volunteer involvement in community charities and civic clubs, and donations to local organizations. In fact, material or subsistence benefits in a then uncertain world were the principal motivators for many of the economic, employment, and market decisions people made.

Beginning somewhere in the 1980s, as indicated in chapter 2, a growing standard of living and unmatched prosperity emerged realigning the public's needs and expectations. Material benefits were becoming less and less important. Jobs were plentiful and the social legislation of the government cushioned any periodic economic downturns.

Prosperity began to be taken for granted. The public, led by the boomer generation, was focusing on higher levels of social needs. They were interested in building and improving the quality of their lives. Education, health, safety, a clean environment, security, dignity, and, most important, some measure of control over their own and their children's future were emerging as the dominant concerns of the public. And these are virtues associated with the middle class.

As Alan Wolfe, a political sociologist, discovered in a survey of the middle class in America, almost all Americans at both ends of the income spectrum believe they are in the middle class. "Despite obvious differences in income," Wolfe reports, "stock-market participation, home ownership and income a middle class mentality has become increasingly ubiquitous in America."[23]

And that middle-class mentality shapes the needs and motivations of the public. While the public supports the need for corporations to make a profit, they also believe it should not be at the expense of the new hierarchy of social needs they have achieved. The American public, according to Wolfe's study, believes in balanced capitalism—"corporations should balance their self-interest with the need to consider what benefits the larger society. For most middle-class Americans," adds Wolfe, "it does not seem unreasonable to think the virtues of capitalism, which they admire, can be reconciled with the virtues of the family and community, which they also admire."[24] Consequently, vast numbers of the American public, and seemingly the public in many other countries as well, insist that corporations treat the community with the same loyalty they want to receive from the community.

Is it any wonder, then, that the Disney Company's promises of 12,000 jobs, 1.86 billion dollars of tax revenues, and thousands of dollars in charitable donations fell on deaf ears? Or that General Electric's threat to move its plastic facility out of Pittsfield if the transformer site and Housatonic river "go[es] Superfund" was met with indifference?[25]

Even low-income communities are no longer persuaded by economic threats to go along with companies' plans. Reacting to the opposition of a neighborhood citizens committee to the building of a cement plant in Camden, New Jersey, the St. Lawrence Cement Company argued that blocking the plant would discourage other businesses from moving to Camden. The citizens committee rejected that argument and continued its protests and successfully prevented the plant from being built.[26]

The lessons are clear: command and control thinking leads to strategies and tactics like DAD that fails when dealing with community disputes. It disrupts relationships with community stakeholders, alienates supporters, and destroys trust between the public and the company.

More significantly, however, command and control thinking disrupts relationships with a wide variety of external stakeholders beyond the traditional community stakeholders. Public officials, international regulators, foreign governments, and worldwide activists are claiming the right to influence a company's license to operate in a variety of areas—mergers and acquisitions, intellectual property, patents and licensing, treatment of employees, and sale of products.

General Electric's failure to obtain approval from the European Commission for the $45 million takeover of the Honeywell Company in 2001 has been blamed on former CEO Jack Welch's arrogance, which personifies the command and control style of relationships. Management theorists, including Warren Bennis, call it a massive failure and embarrassment for Welch.

Microsoft lost its anti-trust case in 1999 because of what Judge Thomas Pennfield Jackson termed the "hubris" of CEO Bill Gates. Gates claimed Judge Jackson has a "Napoleonic concept of himself and his company, an arrogance that derives from Power and unalloyed success with no leavening hard experience, no reverses."[27]

The one conclusion to make is that, in a world where activists are fat, happy, sassy, and successful, DAD does not work. The new rules require a different style of management attitudes, to which we now turn.

CHAPTER 6

Step Three: Use the CACDIC Strategy

If command and control no longer works, what does? Consultation and collaboration. Emotional intelligence. Social skills. Trust relationships. And a stakeholder relations plan.

MOVING MERCK'S HEADQUARTERS

When Merck announced it was moving its headquarters from Rahway, New Jersey, to Whitehouse Station on the western edge of New Jersey, there was understandable concern in both communities. Merck had been located in Rahway since its founding in 1903. For over a hundred years, Rahway served as the company's headquarters, research facility, and manufacturing operation.

The company paid well, had good benefits, and, most of all, had a reputation of treating employees with dignity and honesty. The company had little difficulty in recruiting from in and around Rahway. The city depended heavily on Merck. It was the largest employer and the largest financial supporter of the city and its many programs and services. Many of the company's employees, for example, were volunteers in the public schools.

But the Rahway site was stretching at its seams. It was an aging facility in an aging industrial community alongside one of the busiest stretches of the busiest interstate highway in the country—the New Jersey Turnpike, part of Interstate 95. It is a crowded city of homes, businesses, and large industries struggling to maintain the quality of its services.

Whitehouse Station could not have been more different. It is a small bucolic community not far from the Pennsylvania border. Located in Reddington Township, the total population of the area was at that time 50,000. Land was plentiful, allowing not only for any future expansion that might be needed but also offering a sense of quiet security for an executive and research staff of a large and very successful company.

The move, however, was not without potential disruption. There was a well-recognized psychological contract between Merck and public officials and community leaders. The company's strong support of the local school system and leadership in many of the community's local charities was critical to the ongoing operation of the city. The company needed to maintain those ties and relationships because it would continue manufacturing operations in Rahway.

Second, the employees had ties with the community as well. Many of the services the employees used, such as day care, were not available in Whitehouse Station. Persuading employees to move to Whitehouse Station would have to be a priority.

And third, the company would need to gain a comparable level of acceptance and trust that it enjoyed in Rahway in an entirely new community where it was relatively unknown. Merck planners were aware, too, that the company was about to disrupt the peaceful and traditional routines of a rural community. Merck, after all, represented the fast, bustling industrial east New Jersey, a place many residents of Reddington Township had escaped from. A new psychological contract would have to be developed, one that was agreeable to the residents of Whitehouse Station and the company.

After announcing the move and before any ground was broken on the new facility, Merck began working on these problems. It met with the formal and informal stakeholders (government officials and leaders of community groups and businesses) in Rahway and convinced them that the move to Whitehouse Station would not mean that the company was abandoning its commitments to Rahway. It pledged to continue to support the local institutions at the same level it had given in the past.

The company explained to the employees that it would support services in and around Whitehouse Station. The company would assist in maintaining and improving educational, social, and recreational facilities. Moreover, the company planned to develop an employee day care center to make up for the community's lack of day care facilities.

Prior to the purchase of land, Pat Corretti of the company's engineering staff was assigned to head up the project planning group. He and his group immediately began attending planning board meetings to become familiar with the people and the concerns of the community. They were following the elements of Merck's plan called by its acronym CACDIC—Consult, Announce, Consult again (if necessary), Decide, Implement, and Compensate (if necessary)—and at this point were quiet listeners in the early consultation phase.[1]

Soon Corretti found that he was overwhelmed with questions and the requests for meetings with groups and organizations throughout the county. People had questions about the possible impact of the company on land values and taxes that he and his group did not have the time to adequately answer.

In early 1989, they recruited Gail Fowler, who had been employed by Johnson & Johnson pharmaceutical company. Gail had lived in Reddington Township since 1983 and was familiar with many of the groups and organizations in the community. She was also a volunteer for a few local charities. Her job was to advance the consultation and announcement phases of the project.

Gail developed what she calls "my dog and pony show" and began meeting with organizations throughout the county. "I was out two nights every week talking to community groups. Admittedly, it was exhausting, but necessary."

"Most of the areas of concern," explained Gail, "were related to the impact the company would have on schools and property values. While we were unable to predict property values, we were able to show drawings of the proposed facility, which allayed many of the property value fears. The facility would not loom over the community and intrude on the rural character of Reddington Township. In fact, it would not be visible from the roadway that ran alongside the proposed building." This information was of interest not only to the residents of the site community—Whitehouse Station—but also stakeholders who would be living adjacent to the facility.

Gail also explained that the company promised to work with the community, much as it had in Rahway and in other communities in which Merck facilities are located. "Our goal," she told groups she met with, "is to be partners and participants in improving the quality of life for the community and for our employees."

What was Gail's assessment of the process? "I enjoyed it," she explained. "We worked hard at it. We met with any group that asked, and we also sought out people to speak to. We wanted the community to see us as a valuable asset, a partner, and a good neighbor."

What were the results of Pat Corretti's and Gail Fowler's efforts? First of all, because they had a stakeholder relations plan (CACDIC), they cut in half the time needed to obtain the necessary permits from the community regulators. That savings alone more than compensated for the time, effort, and expenses of Corretti, his engineers, and Gail's dog and pony shows.

Second, the efforts were a publicist's dream: A front page, above-the-fold story in the Metropolitan Section of the *New York Times* headlined, "A Company Move That Hasn't Irked the Neighbors." Praising the efforts of Merck, it also contained comments from officials in both Rahway and Whitehouse Station that could not have been more complimentary. When, for example, another company complained that Merck was having no difficulty in obtaining its permits, the mayor of Whitehouse Station replied, "Merck does its homework."[2]

Third, the effort added to what Merck describes as its community trust account. Merck instructs its facility managers to build up reserves of trust by being honest, open, responsive, and concerned with people and groups in communities in which they operate. Like a bank savings account, Merck officials say, trust accounts can be withdrawn for leverage or collateral when the need arises.[3]

What is the value of these trust accounts? In Albany, Georgia, on July 27, 1995, phosphorous trichloride leaked from Merck's Flint River plant. The leak produced a clearly visible toxic cloud above the plant. Forty-five people were taken to hospitals, and 400 workers were evacuated. Just at that moment, a TV crew was driving by. Reporters quickly began reporting on the incident and interviewing nearby residents, one of whom was the director of a day care center. The potential for damage to Merck's image and its relationships in that community was great, but to the surprise of the reporters, the community was nonchalantly indifferent to the accident. Here are a few comments:

I've never had to be concerned about Merck.

—director of day care center.

I worked down there at Merck. . . . Merck's a good company to be close to.

—James Donaldson, thirty-six-year resident
of the area next to the plant.

They are environmentally conscious and have a good record.
—Scott Robertson, compliance officer with Georgia's Environmental
Protection Department hazardous waste unit.

Fourth, the efforts reaffirmed Merck's decision that managing external stakeholder relationships is not a mystery. It is similar in some respects to managing employee relationships. Both need social skills, and both require that relationships be purposeful and directed. The aim is to create conditions that lead to community buy-in.

For example, at one of its facilities, Merck planned to widen and repair a road leading into the facility. Residents were concerned about the amount of dust and dirt that the construction would cause. Merck compensated the residents by loaning air conditioners to fence-line residents, washing their homes periodically, and providing a gardening service during the construction period.

This decision, based on the empathy characteristic of social skills, generated widespread support for the project. The costs were minimal, and potential expensive costs in delay and litigation were avoided.

BC HYDRO'S USE OF THE CACDIC STRATEGY

On July 14, 1995, BC Hydro, an energy company in western Canada, held a media "briefing" in Maple Ridge, British Columbia, to announce it was expanding its Stave Falls power station to meet the growing power needs of western Canada. The project, claimed the company, would not interfere or take any additional water from the nearby Alouette River and reservoir, a prized recreation area in the community.

Several local residents of the area unexpectedly appeared at the briefing and soon began to dominate the discussion. Gord Robson, a local businessman and leader of a rate-paying association, rebutted the company's presentation and argued that the company was already taking too much water from the reservoir and interfering with the water supply of the Alouette River. "My group," threatened Robson, "is committed to shutting you down. If I have to go to jail to stop you, I'll do it."[4]

Environmentalists in the area, including the Sierra Club's Legal Defense Fund, joined to support the residents. The company's management of the water supply was already damaging the fishing and the ecosystem of the area—a decades old controversy—claimed the Sierra

Club. Water flows into the river varied and at times were as low as less than ten cubic feet per second. The low flows were blamed for the destruction of the fish habitat as well as several floods during rainy periods. One leader of a provincial environmental group asked a BC Hydro official, "Why do residents have to fight so hard for so little?"[5]

The publicity of the meeting strengthened the cause of the residents and environmental groups. BC Hydro's managers quickly recognized that its expansion project along with an upcoming license renewal of another facility were in jeopardy. It had to address these concerns along with the simmering controversy over fishing and flooding if it were going to be able to meet the growing energy needs of the area.

Choosing to adopt a participatory style of planning widely used in city and regional planning, the company called in two consultants, Timothy McDaniels and Robin Gregory, from the University of Vancouver School of Community and Regional Planning.[6] McDaniels and Gregory helped form a seventeen-member committee representing all groups that had an interest or stake in the outcome of the plan. Called the Alouette River Stakeholder Committee, it met monthly over six months. The meetings usually lasted three hours, involving both discussions and listening to reports from the consultants and invited speakers.

Five questions were used to guide the committee's decision making:

- What ends were important to achieve in selecting management alternatives?
- What alternatives can be developed to achieve the objectives?
- What information is needed to identity and define the consequences of the alternatives?
- What trade-offs need to be made in selecting an alternative?
- What alternatives could the committee members support?

Was it successful?

From the company's perspective: A plan was produced that resolved a decades old controversy between BC Hydro and the community over water management issues affecting recreational swimming and fishing. The plan was acceptable to the company and the provincial regulatory commission. In fact, the successful results of the committee's work influenced the provincial government to establish a similar planning process as a condition for licensing utilities.[7]

From the community's perspective: A year later, in 1997, members of the group, which included company representatives, met to celebrate the results of the agreement. It has worked in spades, claimed one news report. The chair of the Alouette River Management Society, Geoff Clayton, charged with monitoring the agreement, was effusive in praising the results. "Hydro's sticking to the agreement to the letter of the law. The water is cleaner," claimed Clayton, "and there was an excellent return of salmon."[8]

From the consultant's perspective: The proof was in the pudding. After fifteen meetings, the committee was able to reach complete consensus on all major issues it was asked to address.

Why did the consultants think the project was successful?

1. It was an open and transparent process allowing observers to attend meetings. Only the committee members, however, were involved in the discussions and decisions.
2. The committee members were able to determine for themselves the values that would guide the planning process and the ultimate selection of the plan objectives, thus assuring a better chance of support for the eventual plan.
3. Information and data were shared openly, freely, and regularly.
4. The alternatives to achieving the objectives of the plan or the details of the plan were selected with the full knowledge of the trade-offs that were being made. It was a guided process that allowed members to either reject or adopt an objective.

The success of the project convinced BC Hydro to use it again when it needed to expand its generating capacity on another river, the Fraser River, which flows south from the coast mountains through the two reservoirs. An even more complex project, it required the setting up of a thirty-one-member committee, representing a wide cross section of stakeholders, including development companies; native Canadians; corrections officials; BC Hydro employees; tackle shops; Ducks Unlimited; government representatives of environment, lands, and parks; housing subdivisions; and tree farms.

Again, a consultant with experience in community planning was hired to facilitate and lead the committee in its development of a recommended operational plan. Similar to the Alouette River project, it was a sequential process involving discussions and accommodations. Eight preliminary objectives were identified. Performance measures were used to assist in the evaluation of alternative solutions to the objectives. The performance measures were used to help the committee reach agreement on the issues and the alternative solutions.

The entire planning process took approximately eighteen months to complete. Both company and stakeholder representatives were entirely satisfied with the process and the results. It eliminated false rumors, generated trust, and improved the quality of decision making, commented the report of the committee. The committee believed that future collaborative planning could be greatly shortened. The experience would help to shorten the learning curve.

But probably the biggest success was universal support of all the recommendations received. Few expected that level of consensus at the outset. While there were some minor disagreements, all thirty-one members endorsed the results.[9]

Admittedly, the BC Hydro process of planning is involved, complex, and lengthy. But think of this: It took less time for the company to obtain acceptance of its water use plans than the time it took the Walt Disney Company to select a site and then withdraw from its plan to develop a theme park in northern Virginia. Also, it was considerably less expensive. The cost of the Alouette River project, for example, was less than $500,000 U.S. dollars, including consultant costs and BC Hydro's staff time. The Disney Company spent close to $1 million for a failed outcome.

SUMMARY

What the Merck and BC Hydro cases demonstrate is the value and effectiveness of the skills in consultation and collaboration. These are not unfamiliar methods for managers, just unfamiliar settings. Thirty years ago, managers began to accept the principles of collaboration and integration in employee relations. They learned that success in employee relations depended upon their skills in creating conditions in which managers and employees worked together to achieve the success of the company. Managers were not, as research in employee relations revealed, giving up their prerogatives of leadership but using new leadership methods to take into consideration the needs of the individuals in the organization when making decisions.

These very same skills, or what some call social skills, are necessary to obtain community or stakeholder buy-in in an era when self-fulfillment needs dominate public attitudes. In each of these case examples, stakeholders were acting to preserve personal values, not economic values. The CACDIC process, used overtly by Merck and implicitly by BC Hydro, responded to these values and attitudes. That is why they were successful. And that is why they are essential in managing a company in an activist world.

What is required, then, is a mind-set and a skill to make working with external organizations and groups a successful cooperative enterprise. It is knowing how to work with others to achieve mutual goals. It is based heavily on developing and using relationships. It demands knowledge of oneself, motivation, conscientiousness, trustworthiness, and a set of social skills, or social judgment.[10]

We will return to this in a later chapter.

CHAPTER 7

Step Four: Who Are Our External Stakeholders and What Do They Value?

In 1984, professor R. Edward Freeman introduced the term *stakeholder*, which he defined as anyone who is affected by or can affect an organization.[1] It has become a helpful tool in analyzing the relationships between individuals and organizations.

It is common to list the community as one among a number of business stakeholders, including employees, shareholders, vendors, and customers. But it is misleading. Communities are made up of a number of subsets of different types of communities. For planning purposes, therefore, the community stakeholder needs to be further refined.

One way to refine the term *community* is to divide it into two major categories—spatial and functional communities. Spatial communities are where people live and companies are located. Functional communities, on the other hand, are made up of people who share some common interest—race, religion, occupation, and membership or association with a group or organization. For that reason they are often called common interest communities.

These are not exclusive categories. People and companies can be located in many different spatial communities at the same time. A person, for example, can live in a city and a neighborhood in that city. People can also be members of many common interest communities.

Let me explain further.

SPATIAL COMMUNITIES

There are five types of spatial communities. One is the *site or facility community*, distinguished by formal geographic boundaries. It is the city, region, and nation in which the company's major facilities are located. Site communities enact laws and regulations that determine where and how a company can operate; it is thus a major definer of a company's license to operate. They also levy taxes and assessments. In return, the community provides services for the company—fire, safety, education, transportation, and the like.

A second type of community is the *employee community*—not the employees themselves, but where the employees live. Many employees live outside of the site area. These employees may, and often do, expect the company to contribute money and volunteer services for NGOs where they live. In fact, it is not uncommon for community-based organizations to expect support from companies that have employees living in their communities. Moreover, the employees have ongoing relationships with key people in their communities who may have influence on issues that can affect the company's freedom to operate.

People who live adjacent to a company facility belong to what is known as the *fence-line community*. Fence-line residents are often affected by a company's operations and its consequences—for example, noise, odors, traffic, and employee behavior.

A company's operations or actions may impact communities far distant from its facility. It may, for example, discharge effluents that affect communities downwind or downstream from a facility. These affected communities are called *impact communities*.

When a company moves out of a community, it has an impact. Some companies have continued supporting NGOs for a limited number of years when they move out of a community. Companies moving into a community also have an impact. It is becoming more and more common for communities to expect companies to demonstrate that they will add value before permission is given to locate a facility.

And then there are communities, generally state/provincial and national capitals, that a company may deliberately make an effort to influence or affect. Some companies, for example, make contributions to NGOs that are in a state capital or the hometown of a key politician.

Finally there is a new community that has no boundaries but is connected by the Internet. It is called the *cyber community* and its effect is illustrated by the Intel case described in chapter 3.

COMMON INTEREST COMMUNITIES

Functional communities, first identified by community organization planners, are made up of people who share a common interest and for that reason are more commonly known today as *common interest communities*. Examples include the health, education, business, social welfare, environment, animal rights, religious, and ethnic communities.

Most common interest communities are composed of organized groups—NGOs that are in business to offer a service and espouse or promote a point of view. The NGOs themselves are made up of professionals, hired individuals who carry out the functions and programs of the NGO, and by volunteers—board and committee members.

Many NGOs may also have a general membership base. Members typically pay a membership fee to support the organization, but they are not active in the running or policymaking of the organization. They may write letters to government officials, companies, or other organizations on behalf of an initiative, and they may also publicly support the organization through fund-raising and demonstrations.

General members can be a source of great influence for an organization because they can be presumed to be acting on behalf of the organization. The larger the membership base, the larger the influence. The National Rifle Association, for example, has a broad and loyal membership base willing to unquestionably support the interests of the organization. This in turn gives the NRA considerable power in influencing legislation because they represent a large voting block.

Greenpeace is another organization that depends on its membership to support periodic actions—boycotts and demonstrations, for example—that limit a company's license to operate. This loyalty is translated into influence that the organization uses to define a company's environmental requirements.

Not all NGOs within a common interest community agree with one another, either about issues or the methods used to achieve the goals of the common interest community. The Society for the Prevention of Cruelty to Animals, for example, is far less militant than PETA.

In addition, there are competitive points of view over solutions to issues and problems. Furthermore, some NGOs are more powerful than others. Medical doctors, represented by the American Medical Association, in the health community often have more influence than pharmacists or nurses. But this is not an absolute. Because of the change in the way medical services are delivered, nursing societies, for example, are increasing their influence in service delivery issues. In other words, nothing can be taken for granted about a nongovernmental organization. Its influence or even its interests can shift drastically as a consequence of changing attitudes, circumstances, and concerns.

Another category of common interest organizations is the spontaneous group that comes into existence to protest the actions of a company and then dissolves once the issue is resolved. Anti-cell tower groups are one example. Because they are spontaneous, they are difficult to predict. Frequently, however, spontaneous groups arise to protest affronts to deeply held values, property values, for example, of cell tower opponents or the values of the small town that are antithetical to mall developments and super Wal-Mart stores.

Even though they are called spontaneous, they sometimes do not dissolve and disappear, particularly if they are successful. The success and the social interaction create satisfactions that people want to maintain. They often go on to fight new issues. An activist group of Vietnam veterans, for example, went on to force nations to outlaw land mines after they were successful in forcing the U.S. government to treat veterans who were victims of Agent Orange. The group won the Nobel Peace prize for its land mine initiatives.

Incidentally, the tendency of organizations to persist even after they presumably have achieved their mission, such as eradicating a disease or solving a social problem, was predicted by a researcher as far back as 1957.[2] Survival is one of the iron laws of organizations, and it is an important point to remember that organizations provide members with satisfaction over and above the achievement of a goal or cause.

LEADERSHIP CATEGORIES

With the exception of the cyber community, there is a formal and informal leadership pattern in all communities. Formal leaders are elected and appointed officials—a mayor; town and city council members; or state, regional, or provincial officials. In addition, there are heads of government departments, school officials, and directors of agencies who all have legitimate authority over a sphere of interest and, consequently, are in a position to influence the outcome of an issue in a community, nation, or society.

There are also informal leaders, sometimes called opinion or thought leaders, who by virtue of their friendships, money, persistence, charisma, skill, and knowledge are able to influence the outcome of an issue. They may be the head of a major corporation, the publisher of a newspaper, a trade union official, the volunteer chair of a major NGO, president of a university, or superintendent of schools.

Because there are so many different types of informal leaders or potential informal leaders, some companies have found it helpful to rely on a categorical scheme to differentiate the leaders.

One category, of course, is the formal leaders, just described. Another is people of influence in mediating organizations. Mediating organizations act on behalf of a particular constituency—local business people, professionals, the elderly, children, cancer victims, religious groups, and homeowners associations, for example. If they engage in a community or societal issue, mediating organization members focus on problem solving and planning. They eschew confrontation and use methods of education, persuasion, and consensus to achieve their ends.

A third category is those who are members of advocacy organizations. Advocacy organizations act on behalf of the needs, aspirations, and interests of a single constituency. They promote the adoption of a single goal—environment, clean water, protection of abused workers, human rights. They promote the needs of the constituency and engage in a variety of methods to achieve their goals—persuasion, promotion, demonstrations, confrontation, contention, and sometimes violence.

Advocacy organizations generally have a widespread membership base. In addition, there are many more people, not members, who share or can be influenced to share an interest in the purpose of the organization. How widespread this group might be is difficult to estimate. Nonetheless, it has to be taken into consideration in estimating the influence of advocacy groups and organizations.

A fourth category of informal leaders are members of self-interest or needs-oriented groups, groups acting on behalf of the members' social or personal needs. Examples include Mothers Against Drunk Driving, organizations of the disabled, clients of social welfare organizations, and organizations of the unemployed. Needs-oriented leaders rely heavily on their organizing skills for influence. They are persistent and achieve many of the goals because of their persistence. They stick with an issue and wear down any opposition because they have a personal stake in the issue outcome.

WAYS OF IDENTIFYING LEADERS

Table 7.1 is useful for identifying stakeholders in developing a stakeholder relations plan. Along the vertical axis are listed the various types of communities that may have influence over a company's license or freedom to operate.

Along the horizontal axis, leaders of the type of community are listed along with brief descriptions of their values and concerns.

The following are six suggestions for identifying the concerns and issues of types of communities:

- *News accounts.* Articles in newspapers—mainstream and alternative—describe appointments of people to heads of organizations. Issues and concerns of government officials are often reported in the media. Public affairs managers, who are commonly responsible for government relations, depend on news reports to keep abreast of changing issues and concerns.
- *The "Walking Around" technique.* Like the highly popular advice in the 1980s for managers to "walk around" the plant to learn the views of employees, the "walk around the community," through attendance at functions in the community, is a quick and easy way to identify people, issues, and concerns.
- *Membership in organizations.* Managers who are active in community groups and organizations are in a position to hear about the issues and concerns of community leaders. They can often probe and follow up on the concerns they hear expressed. In fact, some companies assign managers to become members of community organizations as a way to learn about community concerns.
- *Hosting information meetings.* Some companies host periodic breakfast or luncheon meetings for key leaders in a community. Information about the company and any plans the company may be undertaking that have a community impact are described. Bristol-Myers Squibb, for example, holds meeting of this type in plant communities three or four times a year. The meetings are useful not only for enhancing relationships but are also a sounding board for learning about and addressing rumors or emerging concerns.
- *Attitude surveys.* A number of companies, particularly those in sensitive industries, such as chemical, oil, gas, and utilities, conduct periodic

Table 7.1
Community Assessment Framework

Community Analysis	Leaders	Relationships	Needs	Attitudes	Expectations	Reputation	Concerns

Geographic
  Community
  Fence line
  Region
  Nation
Employee
Impact
  Operations
  Influence
  Entry
  Exit
Common Interest
  Ethnic
  Environment
  Education
  Health
  Relgions
  Etc.							

community attitude surveys. Monsanto, for example, conducts surveys in its plant communities. The purpose of the survey, according to company officials "is to help Monsanto identify and be responsive to local concerns."[3]

There are questions that are based on simple overall opinions. For example: "Do you think (facility name) is very good, somewhat good, somewhat bad, or very bad?"

There are also more detailed questions that ask about the respondents' attitudes about the company's practices toward the environment and its employees, how well the company keep residents informed about the company, and their knowledge of the company's charitable donations to community charities.

- *Community needs assessments.* Needs assessments are conducted primarily to give direction to a company's principal or signature philanthropy programs. It is a way to identify the social needs in a community and the intensity of the needs from the perspective of selected key leaders.

Community needs assessments are also useful because they can reveal the values and concerns of community residents. When people are talking about needs, they are also talking about their concerns and interests. A needs assessment is an organized way for respondents to indicate their concerns.

There are many different types of needs assessments. Some are formal and scientific, carefully conducted, that provide a rich source of information about opinions, wants, and needs in a community. Professional interviewers generally conduct these types of needs assessments. They are expensive to conduct.

A few companies are beginning to conduct informal community needs assessments as a way to learn more about people's attitudes and concerns. The needs assessment may not be as comprehensive or as "scientific" as a formal needs assessment, but it usually reveals enough information to obtain a fairly good picture about the quality of social needs (health, education, recreation, safety, and environment, for example) in a community. Equally important, it is a powerful tool for uncovering the concerns and issues in a community. It is also, as we shall see in the next chapter, an excellent relationship-building technique.

CONDUCTING THE INFORMAL NEEDS ASSESSMENT

Ostensibly, the manager-conducted needs assessment is used as a means for making philanthropy decisions. A manager, for example, makes an appointment with a key leader in a community to ask for his or her opinion about needs.

The manager begins the interview with the following or similar caveat:

> We are interested in learning about the needs in the community so that we can make more intelligent decisions about where we can donate a limited amount of money where it will do the most good. We are interviewing key people, like you, to assist us in making our decisions.

Predictably, and understandably, the interviewees suggest organizations with which they are familiar or those they are associated with. A school superintendent will talk about education needs or the president of the United Way will point to social needs. A few follow-up questions, however, often elicit other needs.

The manager can also pick up cues on the concerns the community may have about the company. Do you think the people in the community are satisfied with the support we give to the community? Does it have a favorable reputation, or does it act in ways that are offensive? Are there unsubstantiated rumors about the company that we should know about? Be especially sensitive to ferreting out unexpressed concerns. They make the most trouble.

Peter Sandman, an expert on risk communication, suggests that managers bring unvoiced concerns to the surface subtly. "I wonder," Sandman advises, "if anyone is worried about. . . ."[4]

It is important to conclude by asking Are there any other key people in the community we should talk to? This is important in order to avoid talking only with people we know or people who are like us. This defeats the purpose of getting to know concerns and issues of the entire community.

A similar observation can be made about searching for key informal leaders in communities and societies. There is a general unwillingness to look beyond the people we know. For this reason, companies often overlook new issues arising in a community that can have important consequences for corporate citizenship strategy making—a point we will return to in later chapters.

There is one final and often forgotten step. People who are interviewed are eager to hear the results. What did other people say? What do others say are the needs in our community? The results can be published and distributed to those interviewed and others in the community. But a far more powerful way to reveal the results is in a meeting of those interviewed. After conducting a needs assessment (usually done every three years), many companies hold a small breakfast meeting or luncheon to announce the results and answer questions. We have discovered that in every instance, when this is done, the company is widely praised not just by the people who attend but by others who have heard about the meeting.

Incidentally, the media likes to attend meetings of this sort. They often end up by writing a highly favorable article about the company. Describing the COMSAT Company's meeting announcing the results of a needs assessment, for example, *The Washington Post* wrote a feature story on the meeting with positive quotes from community stakeholders who attended the meeting.

RAISING EXPECTATIONS

Managers often are reluctant to conduct needs assessments because they believe it will raise unrealizable expectations. Hardly, however, is that the case. In fact, just the opposite is true.

The experience of COMSAT, the satellite company, is generally the norm. When it was trying to decide on a focus for its community involvement programs, it interviewed a number key leaders and government officials for their opinions. One person interviewed was Congressman Edward Markey, then the chairman of the Subcommittee on Telecommunications of the U.S. House of Representatives' Commerce Committee, which had oversight responsibility for COMSAT. Crime and delinquency was the issue selected by Congressman Markey. COMSAT eventually chose education as its priority.

Was Congressman Markey disappointed? Not at all. In fact, he praised the company for reaching out to leaders in the community for their advice.

This illustrates the importance of a needs assessment. It promotes the image that the company cares about its communities. It demonstrates that it wants to contribute to the needs of a community and is willing to listen to what residents have to say about the company and communities. Most important, it promotes *trust*, an essential ingredient of relationship building.

SUMMARY

Social activists in the new society are important stakeholder definers of a company's freedom or license to operate—a point I have repeatedly made. Any company devising a vision and strategy for its corporate citizenship has to begin identifying and assessing those external stakeholders who can have an impact on the license of the company to operate.

What I have tried to present in this chapter is a categorical scheme for identifying the stakeholders and then techniques for assessing the stakeholders' issues, opinions, and concerns. The question a company has to face is not should we conduct an assessment of the external stakeholders, but what kind of assessment technique should we use. In an activist society, a stakeholder assessment is required for developing a stakeholder plan and strategy.

CHAPTER 8

Step Five: What Are the Characteristics of Our Relationships?

There are, as I stated at the outset, five questions a company has to ask as it develops a stakeholder relations plan. The first three were answered in chapter 7.

1. Who are the external stakeholders in all our communities that can influence our license to operate?
2. What do they value?
3. What are their concerns?

We now turn to the fourth question: What is the nature of our current relationships with these stakeholders?

Few managers I have encountered say that the relationships with key people in a community are disastrous. Most, in fact, say they are good. But few are able to define good or even disastrous. And often they confuse attitudes toward the company with relationships. Both are necessary but one (relationships) influences attitudes toward the company.

THE QUICK AND SIMPLE METHOD

In the early 1990s, I was conducting a training program for a half-dozen plant managers of a pharmaceutical company. I asked them to describe their relationships with key people in their communities. Most said, good, positive, okay. When asked how they went about determining this, they all said they based it on informal conversations at civic meetings and social occasions. There were some cranks in the community, everyone admitted, but this was to be expected. All communities have people who are critical of companies for one thing or another.

One manager, however, said that he had set up a three-scale index of key leader attitudes toward the company, ranging from poor through average to good. Those who had any complaints about the company were given a rating of poor. Those who had no comments at all were put in the average column. And those who had anything positive to say were rated good.

It was crude, he said, but useful. Most people rated the company good or average. Only a small percentage gave the company a poor grade. It was a quick and simple assessment, he explained, that gave him a workable idea on what the community thought about the company, and it also helped him to identify issues that could easily be addressed.

How did he make the assessment of the relationships? By getting out into the community, he answered. He relied on what I have described in the last chapter as "the walking around the community" technique.

It served, in effect, as a very simple tool for getting to know people and to promote discussion about the company and its relationships with key stakeholders. It was up to the manager to probe and explore further the initial response of the interviewee's attitudes. This walking-around technique can and should also be divided up among other managers in the company—human resources, finance, operations, and marketing, for example.

ATTITUDE SURVEY METHOD

For some companies, or to follow up on a walking-around assessment, more sophisticated models for assessing attitudes of the public are needed. Monsanto, as I noted earlier, is one of a number of companies that conducts surveys in its plant communities on a periodic basis. The purpose of the survey, according to Monsanto officials and the research company used to conduct the survey, "is to help Monsanto identify and be responsive to local concerns. An understanding of the perspective of local citizens can strengthen [our] community efforts."[1]

There are questions that are based on simple overall opinions. For example: "Do you think (facility name) is very good, somewhat good, somewhat bad, or very bad?" There are also more detailed questions that ask about the respondents' attitudes about the company's practices toward the environment, employees, keeping residents informed about the company, and charitable donations in the community

The survey company Monsanto uses, Market and Communications Research, Inc., however, has also developed an "Intensity Index" that attempts to measure the degree of support or lack of it that residents of a community have toward the company.[2] The index is composed of a series of seven criteria related to specific practices of the company: the environment, waste disposal, reputation as an employer, charitable contributions, confidence in handling a plant emergency, reliability of information the plant provides, and the overall opinion about the company.

The net scores are classified into five intensity groups:

- Supporters: those who take a strong pro-company position on all the criteria;
- Sympathizers: people who lean in favor of the company but are not enthusiastic on one or two of the criteria;
- Straddlers: those who are neither pro nor con;
- Skeptics: those who question the company. While they do not see the company as totally bad, they do not give it the benefit of the doubt on issues;
- Splenetics: hard-core opponents of the company. At least five of the seven questions are against the company.

Survey data such as these are very useful and important pieces of information that every company should have. But they also need to be expanded beyond *community* surveys. There are other stakeholders—stakeholders in state and federal governments, national and international NGOs—that should be part of any company's analysis of its relationships with stakeholders.

However valuable these surveys are, they do not get at the nature of relationships. The questions that have to be asked are: How do you define stakeholder relationships? How can they be measured?

TRUST RELATIONSHIPS

Merck uses the term *trust relationships* to distinguish them from the usual everyday relationships that managers may have with various publics. The goal of every manager is to build relationships of trust.

The manager of the facility has to be perceived by external stakeholders as being trustworthy. Trustworthiness is a function of both character and competence. Managers have character when they are perceived by external stakeholders to have integrity (walking the talk) and maturity (sensitive to the feelings and considerations of others).

Equally important is competence. Managers have to know how to develop trust relationships. It requires a definite skill. And managers have to want to be competent in developing the skills to be perceived as trustworthy. In other words, the skills required cannot be faked. Managers have to be perceived as honest and sincere in their working relationships with external stakeholders.

Trust relationships, Merck cautions its managers, are not established overnight. One meeting with an external stakeholder will not magically and instantly create trust. The process takes time and careful nurturing. There will invariably be a few failures. However, over time, trust can be developed.[3]

Merck had an experience that illustrates the importance of competency in developing trust relationships. The company was in the process of obtaining approval for a medical incinerator. A neighbor who opposed the project took control of a public hearing on the issue and questioned the competency of the company to operate the incinerator by citing information that the company was not always in compliance in running other incinerators and had allegedly caused environmental danger to the property of a fence-line neighbor.

The facility eventually secured the support for the project, but only, Merck explains, after it had spent valuable time and resources on winning back the confidence of the community. The important point that the opponent made was that lack of competence lessens trust.[4]

EMOTIONAL INTELLIGENCE

The development of trust relationships, as I indicated in chapter 6, requires a distinct skill, a social skill, or what Daniel Goleman, a consultant on leadership and an instructor at the Harvard Business School, calls emotional intelligence.[5] Emotional intelligence is the process side of technical or cognitive skills. Most managers can understand the technical qualities of leadership. There are enough books on how to be a manager to answer that question. But what Goleman and others are finding in their studies is that the ability to manage the relationship skills of leadership with employees and colleagues differentiates the successful managers from those who fail.

What we have discovered in our training and research is that the same skills successful managers use in their relationships with subordinates are just as necessary when developing trust relationships with external stakeholders. While technical skills in relationships are important, they cannot overshadow the importance of social skills, and these are the skills managers take for granted when dealing with external stakeholders.

Examples of social skills include:

- Persuasiveness, the ability to influence the opinions of others and to build consensus and support for a company's actions;
- Leadership, the quality of inspiring others to agree on a shared vision and to lead by example;
- Facilitating change, the capacity to recognize the need for change and to enlist others in the goal to bring about change;
- Building bonds, nurturing instrumental relationships;
- Collaboration and cooperation, working with others toward shared goals; and
- Team strengths, being able to work in a team to pursue common goals.

One of the most important of Goleman's social skills for managers dealing with external stakeholders is empathy—the ability to genuinely feel the needs and concerns of people in a community. The manager has to ask: How would I feel in this circumstance? Richard Trabert, the former director of community affairs for Merck, often would challenge managers by asking, if you lived next to our company's facility, how would you like its employees and managers to behave? How would you like to be treated by a plant manager when you had a question about the facility?

Managers who lack empathy, according to Goleman's studies, are labeled arrogant and abrasive. These are the accusations hurled at Jack Welch of G.E. and Michael Eisner of the Disney Company. As I described in chapter 5, both were accused of being insensitive and arrogant in dealing with community stakeholders. If anything, it was the abrasive attitude that led to the failure of their companies to achieve their stated goals and damaged their personal and company reputations.

Another component of Goleman's social skills is the ability to listen and communicate convincingly to external stakeholders. Probably the number one complaint of external stakeholders is: They won't listen to us. Developing trust relationships requires two-way communication.

CACDIC: A SOCIAL SKILL

The CACDIC strategy in working with external stakeholders and described in chapter 6 is an example of the application of social skills. In fact, it depends on competency in social skills for it to be successful. Managers who are not familiar with the elements of social skills appear uncomfortable and insincere in using the CACDIC strategy.

The BC Hydro managers, for example, were comfortable with negotiation and collaboration, and they discovered it was essential to achieving agreement in settling the dispute between the company and its external stakeholders.

The Merck examples are illustrations of the benefits of using social skills to develop and foster trust relationships with key leaders in its plant communities. Merck, in instance after instance, avoids opposition and contention in local communities because it has built up trust that can be called upon when needed. In other words, it works. Managers who develop trust relationships with external stakeholders are more likely to be successful than those who rely on command and control measures.

But does a CACDIC strategy mean giving in to opponents and critics of a company? Not in the least. Our findings suggest that companies that rely on CACDIC and have managers who use emotional intelligence are more likely to be successful than not. The Disney Company, for example, turned its disastrous experience in northern Virginia into a learning lesson. When it made a decision to build a theme park in Orange County, California, it developed a stakeholder relations plan designed to generate community buy-in. The plan was built on working collaboratively with residents and community leaders. The company managers worked on seeking consensus with regulators and residents. It worked. The company had no difficulty in obtaining community approval for the new theme park.

THE STAGES OF RELATIONSHIPS

If we agree that trust relationships are important, what are their characteristics? How can they be described? What goes into developing a relationship?

Two researchers from Capital University in Columbus, Ohio, Stephen Bruning and John Ledingham, took a stab at these questions by comparing how relationships between organizations and the public are made with how interpersonal relationships are developed. They came up with a five-phase process for identifying stages in the development of a relationship between an organization and its stakeholders—key leaders, other organizations, government officials, and others.[6]

First, a caveat. Companies need to be responsive to many different kinds of stakeholders—employees, shareholders, vendors, and government officials, for example. The responses to each of these stakeholders have to be balanced.

While some of the Bruning and Ledingham phases are helpful for describing elements in the stages of a relationship and even as guides in measuring the level of trust in a relationship between a company and an external stakeholder, they have to be considered in context with a company's responsibilities to other stakeholders. Therefore, the Bruning and Ledingham guidelines are just that—guidelines. They help to answer the question: What level of trust does the company have with this stakeholder?

Stage One: The *introductory* phase in the development of a relationship begins when the company provides background information on itself and describes its interest in pursuing a relationship. A plant manager, for example, meets with the mayor to seek his opinion on a needs assessment the company is conducting to determine what nongovernmental agencies should receive donations. The needs assessment approach is a positive way to open up a relationship without making any promises.

Another example: The vice president of human resources in a large multinational company attends an environmental conference involving many environmental advocacy groups. During a break in the meeting, the vice president introduces himself to the presidents of a few of the organizations. He exchanges information on the company and asks to be put on the organization's mailing list. No obligations are suggested. It is a process of getting to know one another. He later writes the presidents thanking them for the material he receives.

Stage Two: In this stage, the *exploration* phase, the focus is on factual issues. Information is exchanged that is substantive in character and defined to reduce ambiguity. During this phase, role expectations are defined and there is an understanding of each other's attitudes, opinions, and interests. Later in this phase, each party will begin to discuss the economic, political, social, and cultural issues that are important to both parties.

The plant manager, for example, may meet with the mayor individually or along with other external stakeholders who were involved in the needs assessment to discuss the results of the needs assessment, explaining what decisions that company has made. The meeting can (should) be used to outline the company's interests and needs for the community. The mayor and other stakeholders should be able to explain their expectations for the community and the company.

In the first example, the human resources vice president may call the contacts he has made with environmental organizations to open discussions on environmental trends. He may also invite representatives of the environmental organizations to participate in a management-training program for general managers. In both instances, there is opportunity to share and discuss issues and concerns of each party in the evolving relationship.

Stage Three: The third Bruning–Ledingham phase in relationship building is the *escalating* phase. The company and the external stake-holder are comfortable with each other. Each has a sense that they know each other's views on social, economic, political, and cultural issues. There are some shared attitudes, opinions, and interests. There is a great deal of comfort and ease in communication. Trust, respect, and openness are characteristics of this phase.

The mayor in our example has no qualms about calling the plant manager to discuss an issue of potential difference. His attitude is, how do we solve this together?

An environmental organization president initiates a call to the vice president for human resources for opinions on business attitudes on potential new legislation. This is not a request for support for the legislation. It is an inquiry question that the environmental organization president is comfortable asking because of the shared relationship.

Stage Four: This stage is termed the *assimilating* phase. It is a phase that companies and external stakeholders can and rarely do fully develop because of different goals and constituency demands. In the assimilating phase, for example, the social, economic, political, and cultural views of the company and the external stakeholder are shared. Each of the parties is able to predict each other's behavior. In fact, one of the parties can make a decision that assumes that the other party prefers.

The fourth phase is characterized by a high level of mutual satisfaction with the relationship. There are, too, feelings of mutual respect and a hope that problems can be solved.

Stage Five: The final, or *fidelity*, stage contains many elements that companies and public stakeholders can rarely achieve, or even try to achieve. Its major characteristic is that there is a public expression of loyalty on the part of the company and its key stakeholders. Obviously, a company cannot balance all the conflicting needs of its many stakeholders by assuring one stakeholder that it has preeminent rights over all other stakeholders, which is what the fidelity stage implies.

SUMMARY

Companies consistently run into trouble with activists because they are not trusted. The intentions of the company are suspect and questioned. Nothing, therefore, is more important in a stakeholder relations plan than a step in the plan for developing trust relationships with external stakeholders. Nonetheless, companies that are judged successful in communities and societies invariably have a plan and expectation that its managers are responsible for developing sustainable trust relationships.

A stakeholder relations plan is not a magic bullet to eliminate opposition to a company's business goals. Positions may be so hardened or opinions so firm that developing trust relationships with some people in some circumstances may not be possible. Without a plan, however, a manager will never know if this is the reason for the opposition. A plan, in other words, is a step, a first step, towards understanding the opinions and concerns of stakeholders. As with all plans it is based on an assumption of hope.

CHAPTER 9

Preparing Managers for the New New Thing

Shortly after the Second World War, Sears Roebuck, as it was then called, was experiencing significant losses in sales and profits. After an analysis of individual store sales, the company discovered a dozen or so stores, unlike all others, that were doing well, very well. Sales were up, and costs were low year after year. These stores were profitable.

The next step was obvious. Why? Why were a few stores successful and the majority unsuccessful? The company discovered that the successful stores differed from all other stores in one significant way. They were organized differently. Failing stores were organized according to the span of control thinking of management at that time. Managers should not be responsible for no more than five to seven employees. The organization chart looked like a pyramid.

The organization chart of the successful stores, on the other hand, was flat. Store managers were responsible for up to fifteen to twenty assistants who, in turn, managed fifteen to twenty employees. Decisions were made easily and quickly. Managers did not have to wait for approval of a request from a half-dozen managers to make up their minds. Thus, managers were able to respond quickly and in a timely manner to any shift in customer attitudes.

Department managers acted like store managers. They had freedom to operate. And they were rewarded because they were treated like managers. Sears quickly adopted the flat structure of organization, as, incidentally, did many other companies. Wide span of control was the way companies should be organized, heralded the management theorists.

A year or so later, Sears reanalyzed their stores. The successful stores were still successful, but the failing stores were still unsuccessful. Again, why?

Unsuccessful stores, the company discovered, made the change in the organization chart, but not in practice. Managers continued to operate informally with the old span of control. They continued to rely on their prior manager for advice and direction even though they were not required to. They knew no other way. They were dependent on the structure, not on the new policy.[1]

The lesson was clear. Changing policy or practice without changing attitudes and behavior does not work.

GENERATING URGENCY FROM THE TOP

When companies begin to shift the focus from a purely community involvement goal to a broader emphasis on corporate citizenship, they encounter the same difficulties. Nothing can be assumed. Managers have different interpretations about the purpose and scope of corporate citizenship, and they are often unaware of the differences. As a result, there are considerable variations on the meaning and purpose of corporate citizenship among managers within the same company. This is what accounts for problems in coordinating policies and practices that eventually can lead to problems with external stakeholders.

One of the first tasks a company has to undertake in preparing managers for assuming corporate citizenship responsibilities is to generate urgency about the need for planning and coordination before any type of training is initiated.

When the Fluor Corporation began to shift from community involvement to corporate citizenship, it started with a one-day retreat for all the top officers in the company conducted by the CEO, Alan Beckman. The Fluor Corporation, located in Aliso Viejo, California, is one of the world's largest and most successful publicly owned engineering, construction, maintenance, and business services companies in the world. It builds highways, manages coal- and gas-power generating stations, builds telecommunication systems for subways, runs copper and gold mining operations, and builds oil wells. It has had offices and operations, in some cases, for over fifty years in North and South America, Asia, Australia, Africa, and Europe.

The company has an enviable community reputation, particularly in California. It has received numerous awards and commendations over its fifty-odd years of operations from local and national organizations for the contributions it made to enhancing the quality of life in communities in which it operates. It was usually the leader in donations and volunteer service. But was that enough? asked Alan Beckman, Fluor's CEO.

In the winter of 2002, Beckman, shortly after being named CEO, began raising questions about the company's community involvement and corporate citizenship practices. He had recently attended a World Trade Organization (WTO) meeting where corporate citizenship was a major topic. Panel presentations and discussions with government leaders and activists associated with nongovernmental organizations challenged the attending CEOs to do more in improving their environmental practices, promoting human rights, and solving health and welfare problems.

After returning from the WTO meeting, Beckman met with Suzanne Hoffman Esber, the director of community relations, for the purpose of planning the annual company foundation meeting. As CEO, Beckman was automatically chair of the foundation. Surprising Esber, Beckman began by asking a number of questions about the company's citizenship practices.

Esber was pleased with his questions, because she, too, had been exploring the issues surrounding corporate citizenship. In discussions with her community affairs colleagues at local and national meetings, she learned that there was a general ferment about corporate citizenship. Expectations were changing and companies were hurrying to adjust and plan for the changes. They were shifting the community relations efforts from philanthropy to a much broader management focus on community and societal issues, and preparing general managers to carry out corporate citizenship practices.

Esber also learned that to be successful in shifting the focus from philanthropy to corporate citizenship, the process for change needed to be driven from the top. The CEO and the senior officers in a company had to be convinced this was necessary. They had to have a common understanding of corporate citizenship and develop a sense of urgency to bring about the change. Fortunately, for Esber, Fluor's CEO was convinced that the shift was necessary.

Beckman decided to alter the usual format of the foundation meeting and convene his direct reports in an all-day retreat to review the company's approach to corporate citizenship. The meeting was initially scheduled for May. Because of schedule conflicts—not uncommon when trying to arrange a meeting of all of a company's senior officers, and particularly so in a global company—it took almost six months to find a mutually acceptable meeting date. Beckman was insistent that the meeting be held at a time when all the direct reports could attend. That sent a convincing message that this would not be a "same old, same old" type of meeting on philanthropy.

It was held August 19, 2002, away from the company's offices at a university conference center. Beckman led the discussion and described the presentations at the WTO meeting. As a consultant from The Center for Corporate Citizenship at Boston College I described the trends and issues in corporate citizenship with examples of what other companies were doing.

The group engaged in a wide-ranging and open discussion of their opinions and experiences in community involvement and corporate citizenship. Many gave examples of problems they saw in responding to the requests and sometimes demands of activist groups. This led to unanimous agreement that the company needed to go beyond the traditional community involvement programs. The meeting concluded with setting up two goals: (1) to invest contributions and other resources in communities that address social and economic goals that benefit both Fluor and society; (2) to improve the visibility of Fluor's impact in the communities in which the company operated around the world.

Two task forces, composed of senior officers, were established. One was a communications task force charged with developing methods for designing ways to inform the entire company about the company's renewed corporate citizenship focus.

The task force decided to use its upcoming fiftieth anniversary of the foundation to promote a worldwide employee voluntarism initiative. The worldwide voluntarism celebration was held in December 2002.

The second task force was charged with planning a citizenship focus for Fluor and the allocation of resources in carrying out the corporate citizenship focus.

As a way to communicate the urgency of corporate citizenship, Beckman's senior officers' meeting was brilliant. By delaying to schedule the meeting until all his direct reports could attend, he sent a message about the importance of corporate citizenship. He was able to move his direct reports to focus on deliverable actions. Little time was needed to generate awareness of the importance of corporate citizenship to the company.

Moreover, the communications task force was able to promote the same sense of urgency throughout the company. Managers around the world were delighted with the change. They saw it as a beginning approach to positioning the company favorably in the communities and nations where Fluor had operations.

The company is continuing its shift in practice and emphasis. Managers are getting the message that corporate citizenship is an important part of the company's mission.

USING WRITTEN DESCRIPTIONS OF CORPORATE CITIZENSHIP

A second tactic is through the distribution of a so-called "white paper," or a copy of an article on corporate citizenship in a business journal to all managers. Journal articles, unfortunately, are often unread. Also, they do not generate any sense of urgency nor do they convince managers that corporate citizenship is any different from community involvement.

One technique is to use a narrative form to explain corporate citizenship. Narratives or articles written like short stories often get the attention of readers. An example is "What is Corporate Citizenship: Conversation with a Manager," written for the Fluor Corporation (see end of chapter). This can be used as a distribution piece or part of material in a training program.

TRAINING

A third tactic is through training. Preparing managers for using corporate citizenship practices in training is becoming increasingly popular and necessary. The Center for Corporate Citizenship at Boston College has seven topics that it uses in the design of a manager training programs in corporate citizenship. Table 9.1, a sample agenda of a training program for corporate citizenship practice containing the topics.

One topic is to obtain an endorsement of corporate citizenship from the CEO for the need and purpose of the training. Obtaining a CEO endorsement is rarely difficult. Most CEOs, similar to the experience of Alan Beckman, are aware of the importance of corporate citizenship in today's environment. What is often the case, however, is that the next level of management is not as enthusiastic. Their

Table 9.1
Sample Agenda

AGENDA **Making the XY Corporation a Leader in Corporate Citizenship**	

A Conference on Corporate Citizenship
For XY's general managers
June 24, 2004
State University Conference Center

MONDAY

8:00 to 8:30 A.M.	**Welcome: Objectives and Overview of Seminar**
	Welcoming remarks • Joe McKenney, Executive Vice President • John Connors, Vice President, Corporate Citizenship and Community Relations **Introduction and conference overview** • Lois Moody, Boston College
8:30 to 10:00 A.M.	**What is corporate citizenship? The XY approach** How do we define corporate citizenship for the XY Company? (Table Activity)
10:45 to Noon	**Who are our stakeholders: at the community level** (manufacturing and sales facilities will present findings from pre-seminar community survey) **At the global level** (discussion of global stakeholder issues led by EVP)
Noon to 1:00 P.M.	**The psychological contract** Preparation for roundtable session. Identifying the implicit expectations of stakeholders.
1:10 to 2:00 P.M.	**Roundtable presentation from three stakeholders** Environment (Director of state environmental protection agency) Legislative (mayor) Philanthropy (Volunteer president of Community Foundation)

Table 9.1 Continued

2:10 to 4:30 P.M.	**Case study assignments** Three cases highlighting corporate citizenship issues; viz., 1. Public education and recruitment of skilled labor force; 2. Neighborhood opposition to plant expansion; 3. Potential boycott of company's outsourcing programs. Participants are required to develop a response to the problem, which will be critiqued by a panel of citizen leaders and representatives of an advocacy group.
6:00 P.M.	**Dinner presentation: What defines a company's citizenship reputation?** John Ready, author, "Reputation Analysis. What Does the Public Say About Our Company and How Do We Find Out About It?"
TUESDAY	
8:30 to 10:00 A.M.	**Designing strategies for XY's corporate citizenship: workshop assignment** Three separate groups will devise a corporate citizenship strategy based on an assessment of XY's current citizenship program and policy using the analysis outline. Group one will develop a global employee volunteer strategy. Group two will develop a beyond compliance environmental strategy. Group three will develop a marketing strategy of corporate citizenship.
10:15 to Noon	**Presentation and discussion of strategies to planning jury** Fred Tirrell, HR; Fred Hayes, V.P. Legal Affairs; and Walt Nagle, CFO.
Noon to 1:15 P.M.	John Carley, Editor; Issues letter, trends and issues affecting companies.
1:30 to 3:00 P.M.	**Best practices: What are other companies doing?** Panel discussion with three companies in our industry chaired by Julie Hardin, Director of Industry Association

(continued)

Table 9.1   Continued

3:00 to 4:30 P.M.	**Ways of planning and evaluating corporate citizenship practices and programs** Lee Bajek, Boston College
4:30 to 5:30 P.M.	Explanation of planning format for Wednesday morning.
6:30 to 7:30 P.M.	Dinner
7:30 to 9:00 P.M.	**Planning time** Participants begin designing planning and evaluation assignments

WEDNESDAY

8:30 to 9:00 A.M.	**Continuation and completion of planning time**
9:15 to 11:00 A.M.	Presentation of planning and evaluation of corporate citizenship methods for XY.
11:00 to Noon	**Next steps and action planning** Developing a time schedule for implementation.
Noon to 1:00 P.M.	**Lunch and adjournment**

energies are directed to achieving business goals associated with their responsibilities.

The importance of obtaining the support and endorsement of senior managers cannot be overemphasized. Here is an example of the way the Sprint regional telephone companies obtained the endorsement of a senior manager and, at the same time, recruited an internal ally for community involvement. In the 1990s, Sprint was setting up training programs for managers of its telephone companies in the Pennsylvania region. The focus of the programs at that time was on community involvement.

A vice president was recruited to speak at the opening dinner meeting to endorse the training program and describe its importance to the future success of the company. He was not eager, but a letter from the CEO *helped* persuade him to carry out the assignment. The training program planning director met with the vice president to assist him prepare his talk. She was able to convince him to speak to other vice presidents in other regions and at corporate headquarters to get ideas for his talk. In the process, the vice president, deliberately on the part of the community relations manager, became a target of the training. His discussions with other vice presidents, along with discovering what other telephone companies were doing in community involvement, helped him to give a creditable talk.

At the initiation of the director of community relations, the vice president's talk was reported in the company newsletter. He indirectly became an advocate and champion of community involvement.

Because there are different interpretations of corporate citizenship, a second topic in training is to provide a session or two that helps the participants arrive at a common understanding of corporate citizenship for the company. The "What is corporate citizenship?" session on the sample agenda (Table 9.2) is used to achieve this goal.

A third topic in training is developing ways to allow external stakeholders to be involved in the training. Some companies invite community leaders to participate in roundtable discussions. Others actually invite stakeholders to critique a project developed by participants as part of a case assignment. This provides opportunities to understand and learn the motivations of external stakeholders. People learn best when they are engaged in an experience. That is why internships and fieldwork are used in graduate education. While not as effective, case assignments can be substituted to approximate an experiential process.

Merck is a company that uses cases and problem-solving assignments in its training of facility managers. The cases are brief and problem focused. Although composites of real incidents and events, they are fictitious. The managers are divided into groups (normally three or four groups of seven to nine managers), given directions on solving a community problem, and then asked to report back to the total group, or a "jury" of experts, according to a prewritten format.

In the community problem-solving assignments, the managers give their reports to actual community representatives—mayors, city council members, board members of the United Way, representatives of environmental organizations, newspaper reporters, and directors of social service agencies, such as the Urban League. They ask questions designed to challenge the managers and then critique the reports. There are usually three community leaders on each juror panel.

This method helps managers grasp the thought processes of the community leaders and activists. In some instances, city council members and environmentalists have explained that their critiques were based on what their constituents would have them make. "I have to be responsive to my constituency," commented an activist at one of the training sessions. "Otherwise I would not be able to keep my job as chairperson."

This type of session provides opportunities to describe the importance of social skills in relating to stakeholders. In some instances, an additional session is used to explain the elements of emotional intelligence. Case examples can be used to outline the critical steps. It is very helpful to use a facilitator in such a session

Topic four, is a session on the "psychological contract" between a company and its external stakeholders. The purpose of this topic is to assist managers in developing ways to anticipate emerging issues and concerns. The psychological contract, explained in chapter 11 is a tool in managing corporate citizenship.

A fifth topic of The Center's manager training programs in corporate citizenship is to design cases and assignments that engage the participants in solving a problem or in designing a plan that they will likely implement when the training is over. A training program that engages managers in designing plans that they use in the future creates commitment to the plan. Note that in the sample agenda, the participants are also asked to present projects findings to a "jury" of their peers.

This is another means for creating commitment to follow through on implementing a project. It is a public presentation, and managers tend to follow through on commitments they have made publicly.

Richard Trabert, the former director of community affairs for Merck, engages managers in his training programs to begin developing an external relations plan as an assignment. The external relations plan, explains Trabert, details a facility's role, objectives, and activities in the communities in which it operates.

The goal of the external relations plan, according to Trabert, is to answer three questions: (1) How can we improve the trust relationships between the facility and the community? (2) How can we help improve the quality of life in the community? (3) How does our business affect the community?[2]

A sixth topic is using best practices examples. It has been found helpful to provide a session on best practices, examples of successful corporate citizenship programs and practices. It gives managers an opportunity to compare their own practices with others, creating an incentive to change and improve their own practices. In some cases, companies invite managers from other companies to describe their programs, thus paving the way for meaningful discussions.

A variation of best practices, or peer learning from best practices, is what Mark Leidy, executive vice president of manufacturing of Monsanto, calls "stealing shamelessly with pride." Managers of the company are provided with opportunities to describe how they have handled issues and concerns about the corporate citizenship practices of their companies and facilities.

Topic seven, is to use outside speakers to discuss corporate citizenship. It is best to involve outside "experts" at a luncheon or dinner meeting. Speakers' presentations should be short—rarely more than fifteen or twenty minutes. TV programs have conditioned audiences to fifteen-minute attention spans. After that, the mind wanders and the audience is lost.

ONGOING COMMITMENT TO THE NEW NEW THING

Coordination of practices is achieved by continual reinforcement. We have discovered that companies with effective corporate citizenship reputations make reporting on issues and concerns a part of management meetings along with the usual monthly reporting on health and safety practices.

It also helps to reinforce the corporate citizenship vision of the company. But it has to done in a way that continues to generate urgency and commitment to corporate citizenship. For a number of companies, the stealing shamelessly with pride technique is a useful and effective way to guide these discussions. Managers are provided with opportunities to describe how they have handled issues and concerns about the corporate citizenship practices of their companies and facilities. Managers are much more likely to adopt practices learned from the peers than from trainers or outside educators.

GENERATING THE CORPORATE CITIZENSHIP CONDITION LETTER

The corporate citizenship, or as it is sometimes called, a social issues condition letter, is similar to the condition letters sales and marketing managers prepare on a periodic basis. Sales condition letters, for example, describe the condition of the market, emerging consumer trends, changes in purchasing habits, and any changes in the practice of competitors.

Corporate citizenship condition letters are similar. They are used to report on emerging trends and issues, brief statements of concerns of thought leaders and activist groups, and a general sense of the attitudes of the public in one or more of the company's communities. The typology described in chapter 7 is a helpful format for condition letters. The purpose of the condition letters is to avoid surprises and to anticipate issues and concerns. Certainly, the one characteristic of the problems faced by the Disney Company and G.E., described in chapter 5, is "surprise." Neither Disney nor G.E. managers expected the reaction of the public to their intentions.

Once a company is taken by surprise in a community, it is frequently playing catch-up. It is constantly racing after rumors and criticism. That can be avoided with condition letters. At the very least, it is a way to assist managers to maintain a focus on social issues.

SUMMARY

Preparing managers for their new functions in corporate citizenship cannot be left to chance. They have to be prepared. They have to be trained. Companies do not have to reinvent the wheel of corporate citizenship training. Many companies, some cited in this chapter, have developed successful programs that can be used as models for establishing a successful manger training program.

What Is Corporate Citizenship: Conversation with a Manager

"What is corporate citizenship?"

I was asked this question recently at a philanthropy reception by Ray Dodd, a colleague and executive vice president of a hi-tech manufacturing company in the southern part of the state. We met at a Boston College Center for Corporate Citizenship seminar four or five years ago. We were the only operating managers at the seminar from Ohio. We became friends and kept in touch with each other by phone or e-mail and occasionally met at statewide functions.

"What do you think it is?" I asked.

"I can't believe it. You sound like an academic or psychiatrist, parrying a question with a question. But I have to agree it is a good way to start.

"Some of our senior managers were wrestling with this issue a few weeks ago. It was a spirited conversation provoking a lot of thought and discussion but no answers. We concluded we needed to find out more about corporate citizenship before we decided what our company should be doing. Running into you is a lucky accident.

"I heard your company just introduced a corporate citizenship strategy. You can tell me how it went.

"We know it includes community involvement," continued Ray. "And we think we're doing a good job here. At least the community and our employees think so. We get a lot of praise for our philanthropy and our employee volunteer programs."

"What else did they say?" I asked.

"Environment—protecting the environment, developing manufacturing processes that do not violate environmental laws and regulations. We were unanimous on this.

"We have a good environmental program and record. Our health, safety, and environment managers see to that.

"But we are uneasy. We were concerned about future expectations. I recently learned that companies that lump environment with health and safety are coming under heavy criticism, particularly in other countries where we have facilities. The talk now is environmental sustainability. That goes beyond the usual compliance issues. It is becoming more and more complex.

(continued)

"We said ethics is another element of corporate citizenship. We need to be ethical in our relationships, and operating our business ethically is a way to demonstrate our social responsibility, I guess."

"Continue," I said. "You're on a roll."

"We also talked about human rights. We shouldn't do business in countries or societies that violate our sense of human rights. Of course, we couldn't agree on what that was. We recognized outrageous cases, Iraq, Iran, Myanmar. But then someone asked about China, and that really got us going.

"We are doing business in China. And we will probably do more. China represents almost one-fifth of the world's population. It can't be ignored. It persecutes people for their religious beliefs, which is a human rights issue.

"Also we're planning to build a plant in Cuba. We're concerned about the reaction we will get from Cuban immigrants. Please, incidentally, respect our confidences in this.

"How do we proclaim we are opposed to violating human rights and still do business in countries that are repressive? We had no answer. And we better find one. Human rights groups are asking us for information on our China businesses.

"This brought up the question of wages and working conditions in third world countries," continued Ray. "We have a couple of plants in Mexico and one each in Indonesia and the Philippines.

"The wage scale is a lot lower than what we would pay in the U.S., but that's why we are in these countries. It's for competitive reasons. Then, too, these wages are far superior to what they once were paid or could get from companies in their countries.

"We try to provide decent working conditions. But one problem is the managers in these countries have a different concept of what we mean by decent working conditions and how you treat employees. They have their own customs and values. A lot different from ours. And it's difficult trying to persuade them to change.

"Transparency. We certainly agreed that we should be open and honest in our relationships with governments and people in communities. And I think we have been. A major component of our community relations strategy is to develop 'relationships of trust.' And trust begins with honesty.

"But transparency seems to mean something different in corporate citizenship. Certainly we can't share information that would benefit our competitors. Discuss business plans and strategies, for example.

"And we don't think it's fair to provide information on our profit margins. There are groups, we understand, demanding that companies disclose both the costs of producing a product or service and the amount charged to the customer.

"It's very vague. In fact, that was the general conclusion of our discussion. Corporate citizenship is vague and ambiguous. We can't seem to get a handle on it. While we want to be a good corporate citizen, no one can tell us what that is. It is frustrating.

"Look, I answered your question," said Ray. "Now answer mine. What is corporate citizenship?"

"One more question," I said.

"Oh, great."

"What prompted the discussion about corporate citizenship?"

"The CEO. She attended a World Trade Organization meeting in New York and corporate citizenship dominated the discussions. Heads of non-governmental organizations gave presentations at one session. They were critical of corporations. Some so critical and hostile that they turned off many in the audience.

"But they made their point, according to our CEO. She said we'd better have a strategy if only to answer questions from stakeholders in our plant and service communities. I was asked to head up a committee of vice presidents to prepare a report on the company's response to corporate citizenship demands.

"Now, forget the academician role, and tell me what you think corporate citizenship is?"

"Alright. Let me tell you what we discovered in our planning and some information we got from other companies.

"Many in the company and other companies shared your sentiment that corporate citizenship is ambiguous. It is difficult to describe and define. On top of that, many different terms are used— responsible citizenship, corporate social responsibility, corporate social responsiveness, community investment, and community relations, for example. This only adds to the confusion.

(continued)

"Part of the difficulty is that we're used to making programmatic responses to external affairs. When Reagan unleashed what we've come to see as the modern era of community relations in the U.S. by asking corporations to become involved in communities to make up for the cuts he was making in social programs, we were all forced to expand our giving programs. All sorts of nonprofits were banging at our doors. And as the demands continued to grow, we like you started developing volunteer programs. And then it was partnerships with schools. And health fairs. And economic development. We were scrambling to get ahead of the activist demands, just as I suspect you were.

"We initially made the mistake of confusing community involvement with corporate citizenship. In answer to the criticism we were getting from some noisy nonprofits, we gave high profile grants to social agencies and schools. We organized a world volunteer day.

"It cut no ice. We even got criticized for trying to bribe the community for our supposedly poor environmental practices. We've had no criticism or complaints from the state environmental protection agency. None. Still we were criticized.

"When we analyzed it, we saw we were resting on our community relations reputation, particularly our employee volunteer programs.

"And another mistake. As we began to expand our community involvement, we turned these programs over to managers, community relations managers. A form of outsourcing in a way. The headache was gone. There was someone in the company who was in charge of dealing with all the nonprofits asking for more and more money.

"But who do you put in charge of transparency? Human rights? Nonexploitive wage and working conditions in developing countries? Ethics?"

"We have an ethics manager," said Ray. "He's a lawyer and works out of the legal department."

"So do we. What does he do?"

"Compliance, I guess," answered Ray. "Makes sure we're not violating any laws. Oh, they also have an ethics pamphlet that is mailed out once a year and distributed at orientation sessions for new managers."

"You have an environment manager, too, who probably also handles health and safety."

"We do. And we have EHS managers at all our facilities. They work with the Local Area Planning Committees in their communities as part of the of Sara Title III requirements."

"Do these people talk to each other?" I asked.

"Who? You mean EHS and Ethics? I don't know. Come to think of it, I don't think the EHS managers and community relations managers talk to each other even though both have similar community programs and advisory committees."

"That's what we found. We had a variety of different functions that were related to corporate citizenship—community involvement, environment, ethics, public affairs. We discovered, too, that there were a number of corporate citizenship activities that are not part of any function or department in the company—transparency, human rights, and diversity. Diversity is one you didn't mention.

"We also found we weren't involved in defining these functions. The activists were. And they kept changing the goal posts. That's what creates the ambiguity.

"Okay. What did you do?"

"I'm getting there.

"First of all, it's not about developing programs. It's about behavior. How a company behaves in a community and in a society as it goes about doing the business that it is in. Do we, for example, have honest, open, and respectful relationships with stakeholders, including activist groups, with whom we disagree? Are we truthful in what we say and do? Are we sincerely interested in protecting and sustaining the environment for our children and grandchildren? Do we make sure that our employees, regardless of where they live in this world, are treated with dignity and respect? Are we willing to forsake profits to respect the integrity of the company?

"That's all well and good," said Ray. "And it sounds peachy. In fact, we could put those pieties in a lovely little pamphlet. But nothing would change. They don't tell us what to do when faced with a corporate citizenship issue. Let me give you an example.

"Some twenty years ago, when I was a plant manager in Indiana, we ran into a pollution debacle not of our own making. A chemical

(continued)

we used in a manufacturing process left a residue that had to be deposited in a designated waste site.

"We used a local waste company to haul it away once a month. It usually amounted to a dozen barrels.

"The residue gave off an odor that was not offensive, but it was apparently a nuisance to our neighbors living adjacent to the plant. In fact, the mayor told me she was getting complaints when I ran into her at a Rotary meeting. I told her I would look into it.

"I talked to the employee in charge of disposing waste, including the chemical waste. He explained it was difficult to mask the odor. One solution, he suggested, was to pick up the waste more often. That would have some effect on reducing the smell.

"Then he also revealed that he had questions about the waste company. He heard rumors that the waste company was illegally dumping the chemical residue into the local landfill. They were supposed to be depositing it in a landfill a few hundred miles away that was designated for chemical waste disposal.

"That was something I did not want to get involved in. Out of sight, out of mind. I did agree to increase the pick up of the waste to twice a month. That would placate the neighbors. It seemed to solve the problem. For the moment.

"An environment watchdog group—actually a local group of fifteen or twenty residents—caught the waste disposal company dumping the waste in the local landfill. They also discovered they were dumping the waste in out of the way fields in another county.

"We were identified as the source of the chemical. And, of course, we were blamed. Try as we might, it was difficult for us to disassociate ourselves from the vendor. We took a lot of heat and it took up a great deal of my time.

"We eventually changed our manufacturing processes that eliminated the chemical. It cost us over a million dollars.

"On top of that, I lost all credibility with the mayor. She was steamed.

"I'm telling you about this incident," continued Ray, "because I also told it to the committee. And as I was telling it I began to see it in a different light."

"What did you learn?" I asked.

"I would do things differently today. I would investigate different manufacturing processes to avoid using a chemical that was offensive and a nuisance.

"I would follow up on the suspicions of the employee who warned me about the waste company. We have a responsibility to the people in our towns and our employees to do the right thing. The vendors we use are acting on our behalf. We should make sure they act as responsibly as we do.

"I'm embarrassed, now, I told the other vice presidents, that I gave the employee the impression we didn't care what the waste company was doing. "The 'it's not our problem' mentality is outdated and wrong. It is our responsibility."

"What a great story!" I said. "We came to a similar conclusion after our study.

"Implementing a corporate citizenship strategy requires a different mentality. A different way of thinking.

"And, Ray, we found that that's the most difficult thing to accomplish. But you can do it. It takes time and most of all the commitment from the CEO."

"Can you come," asked Ray, "to talk to our vice president strategy committee? I think they would benefit learning from your experience."

"Okay. Call me tomorrow and we'll set a date."

CHAPTER 10

The Stakeholder Relations Plan

The preceding four chapters form the basis of a stakeholder relations plan. At this point, it is useful to sum up the elements of the plan before discussing issues of strategy and structure.

There are two types of stakeholder relations plans. One is an annual external relations plan that sums up the overall assessment of the company's relationship status among key organizations and thought leaders, including activist groups in its various spatial communities. This plan can be described in a two- to three-page "Social Issues Condition of Communities" letter.

Other stakeholder relationship plans are developed whenever the company is engaged in intervening into the community to obtain approval for change in the way the company will be operated.

There are nine steps in the development of an external stakeholder relations plan:

1. Specify the spatial communities that are definers of the company's license to operate. These include the site, fence line, employee, cyber, and impact communities. Remember that the site community includes facility, regional, and national communities.
2. Specify the common interest communities that are definers of the company's license to operate.
3. Identify the key organizations and key thought leaders among the spatial and common interest communities. Identify the community issues, needs, and concerns of each stakeholder group.
4. On the basis of a simple scale of high, medium, or low, estimate the level of influence of the key organizations and key thought leaders.

5. Determine the level of the company's relationship with the key organizations and key thought leaders.
6. Assign managers to organizations and key thought leaders for the purpose of developing trust relationships and for assessing their issues and concerns about the company.
7. Develop an external relations plan based on the issues and concerns of the key stakeholder groups.
8. When the company is considering changes in operations and plans that may have community implications, develop an impact external relations plan.
9. Submit quarterly social-issues condition letters to supervisor. Supervisors should develop summary social-issues condition letters that are forwarded to a senior officer responsible for the company's external stakeholder relations.

CHAPTER 11

The Site Community Strategy: A Responsibility of the Facility Manager

In 1982, Rev. Jesse Jackson threatened Anheuser-Busch, the giant beer company, with a nationwide boycott if it did not improve its performance with the black community. Jackson claimed that 15 percent of Anheuser-Busch's customers were black; consequently, 15 percent of its employees should be black, 15 percent of its deposits should be with black-owned banks, 15 percent of its wholesalers should be black, and 15 percent of its purchasers should be from black vendors.[1]

Jackson was confident he would succeed. He had successfully negotiated similar, what he called, "reciprocity" agreements with Coca-Cola, Seven Up, and Heublein. Anheuser-Busch looked like an easy target.

The threat was a frightening prospect for Anheuser-Busch. The company was the leader in the beer industry. Nonetheless, the beer industry was highly competitive, and consumer confidence in the company as well as its products was important. But black community leaders and organizations in St. Louis and other cities where the company had major facilities rallied to the company's defense. The company's record was superb, they explained. Over 19 percent of its employees were black. The company deposited $10 million in minority-owned banks and purchased $18 million in products from minority suppliers.

The company had two African American board members. One was the vice president for corporate affairs who was in charge of the relationship building and community practice programs. The company supports a number of organizations working with minority youngsters. It has an urban scholarship program designed to foster the growth and development of inner-city youth. It supports mentoring programs in public schools. It invites community leaders to company events and has a variety of informal programs to build relationships with community leaders and groups.

The boycott failed. In fact, it never got off the ground. In September 1983, less than a year after Rev. Jackson announced the boycott, it was called off. Rev. Jackson praised the company's relations with the black communities. The calling of the boycott, said Rev. Jackson, was "attributable to a failure of communication."[2]

What this incident illustrates is the value and necessity of a community strategy. In an activist society, the community is the dominant definer of a company's license to operate. No company, consequently, can operate freely today without a strategy that generates consent and acceptance by a community's formal and informal leadership.

A company also needs a global or societal strategy, which will be described in the next chapter.

PURPOSE OF THE SITE COMMUNITY STRATEGY

"Companies," warned Richard Evan, former vice president of Amoco "operate only with the permission of the community. And," he added, "that permission has to be earned."[3] And it is earned chiefly by developing trust relationships with key community stakeholders for the purpose of maintaining the company's license to operate.

Many companies now use the principle of the Neighbor of Choice[4] to frame their site community strategy. Based on an analysis of the expectations of site community stakeholders, it provides a basis for planning and operating site community strategies and programs.

A company needs to behave in ways that promote and build trust between it and all its external stakeholders. It is not unlike the relationship between companies and consumers. Consumers' expectations for quality products and services continue to increase. Successful companies strive to go beyond those expectations. They develop behaviors that promote the reputation of their products. Many companies use the metaphor "supplier of choice" as a principle to guide this kind of behavior. In turn, they develop courses of action or strategies to become a supplier of choice. Quality programs are examples.

Similarly, the metaphor "employer of choice" is a behavioral principle to guide strategies to attract and retain the best and brightest employees. Wellness programs, work and family accommodations, and the community reputation of the company are strategies to make a company an employer of choice.

Investors are also changing expectations. They want to invest in companies that are responsive to environment needs and ethical behavior. In other words, successful companies have to act in ways that make them a supplier of choice, an employer of choice, and an investor of choice. Now they have to be a neighbor of choice.

The term *neighbor of choice* refers to the reputation of the company in the community. Is the company a necessary and desirable asset? Is it sensitive to community concerns? Does the company operate its facilities in ways that demonstrate a respect for community concern? Are the company's actions consistent with its message? Does it support and contribute to improving the quality of life in the community? Does the company respect the community's values and traditions? Does it live up to its commitments? Are its actions predictable?

In other words, can the company be trusted? Trust is the critical question and the underlying definition of being a neighbor of choice. Trust is necessary in developing a positive reputation. Where there is trust, there is respect, a willingness to take someone's expressions and actions at face value. There are no suspicions, no hidden agendas. Problems and difficulties can be worked out. People who trust each other understand that mistakes can happen, that people will work to correct mistakes.

Trust cannot be controlled or manipulated. It is based on a company's reputation, which in turn is based on perceptions—how others, particularly critical stakeholders, view the company. Unlike a company image, therefore, a company's reputation cannot be manipulated, managed, or given a "spin."

Trust, however, is a perishable commodity that needs to be nourished and sustained. It can never be taken for granted. It can never be assumed. It is, as the Canadian Imperial Bank of Commerce advises its manager in its community relations manual for all employees, "earned and comes from being consistent and dependable in doing what we say we will do. Building trust takes time and builds slowly as we begin to show proof of results."[5]

Trust is measurable. Companies that are trusted tend to have respect and good community reputations. They are the admired companies. *Fortune* magazine's listing of the top ten companies, for example, consistently is composed of companies with excellent community reputations.[6]

THE PSYCHOLOGICAL CONTRACT

What guides the development of site community strategies are expectations—expectations site communities have for a company and the expectations that a company has for its site communities. We call this the "psychological contract."

The psychological contract, unlike a social contract, which is explicit, contains both the explicit and unwritten expectations that companies and their internal stakeholders have for each other. Although the implicit expectations remain beneath the surface of relationships, they are dynamic in character. They are continually changing and frequently unacknowledged. They are a manifestation, too, of the ideals that one party to the contract has for the other.

Developed by Harvard Business School professor emeritus Harry Levinson as a method for managing supervisory relationships, it is also an important—in fact, I would say, a critical—concept for managing stakeholder relationships.[7] I have explained this in an earlier book on corporate community relations, but it deserves a summary explanation here.[8]

When a manager joins a company, explains Levinson, he or she brings along specific needs, some of which are met and described in a job description. Others, a manager's hopes, aspirations, and ideals, are not. A manager wants also to advance within the company, develop new skills and knowledge, form collegial and friendly relationships with other managers, and, above all, be treated with dignity, fairness, honesty, and respect.

The company, too, has both written and unwritten expectations for its managers. The explicit expectations are contained in the job descriptions or its policies, benefit plans, and department or company mission statements, and are discussed in performance reviews. The implicit expectations include loyalty, trustworthiness, and dependable work habits. A company also expects its managers to go beyond the job descriptions in crises or emergencies, not to embarrass or scandalize the company, keep the company's secrets, respect confidentiality, support and protect colleagues, and work pleasantly and cooperatively in teams.

These combined expectations form the psychological contract. Although implicit expectations are unwritten, each party tacitly assumes that such a contract exists, and each expects the other to act in keeping it. "When," Levinson writes, "one or another party to the contract unilaterally violates it, then the other reacts with all the anger and frustration that usually follows an experience of being treated unfairly."[9]

There is a similar psychological relationship between a company and its site communities. Just as employees have expectations for a company of how they want to be treated, so, too, do communities. They have ideals of how they want the company to treat them and the communities in which they live.

As we saw in chapter 3, "The Faces of Activism," people want to live in communities that are clean, environmentally safe, friendly, and cooperative. The communities are the places to raise families, to grow businesses, and to survive and prosper. People work together informally and in organized groups to achieve these ends. While these are aspirations and may not be fully achievable, there is the expectation that everyone is seeking to achieve them in common. There is a reciprocity of trust—a common basis, a common set of values—that joins people together to live the good life.

There are recognized values that are held in common—a company needs to remain competitive and a community needs to be treated honestly and fairly—and there will be a mutual attempt to make each other successful in achieving these aims.

When a significant change takes place—a company introduces a manufacturing process that has environmental implications; it is discovered that a company is leaking chemicals into a local river; a company moves an operation off shore, thus reducing employment by two-thirds; a company enters into bankruptcy and gives a multimillion dollar settlement to the discharged CEO—a conflict between the company and its site community becomes manifest. Stakeholders become angry, protests and demonstrations occur, and companies get sued.

Communities and other external stakeholders may also make decisions that can violate the expectations that a company has held. A community may introduce regulations governing the future plans of a company. Organizations may call for a boycott of a company because of its wage policies. An organization introduces a proposal to penalize firms that move operations off shore.

During the early 2000s, for example, there was a growing uneasiness in developed nations that companies were exporting or outsourcing jobs to developing countries to the detriment of the national interests. Companies were also moving to countries that had more favorable tax rates than their own nations. For many, this was a loyalty issue. Companies moving off shore were disloyal.

At the same time, companies were complaining that communities and societies refused to understand the new economic problems of the new millennium. Global competitiveness was growing and creating a whole new set of problems for companies. They had to reduce costs to compete in the global economy. The psychological contract was broken and it became a vitriolic campaign issue in the 2004 presidential election.

Assessing both the explicit and implicit expectations is critical in developing both a community strategy and programs for implementing the strategy. Methods for identifying expectations are described below.

Companies also need to develop internal mechanisms for identifying the expectations the company has for communities. It is often forgotten that the psychological contract is based on both company and community expectations.

THE ESSENTIAL PROGRAMS OF THE SITE COMMUNITY STRATEGY

At a minimum, a company must have five essential programs for a successful site community strategy. One is a program that is aimed specifically at building trust relationships. The second is a philanthropy program. The third is an employee volunteer program. The fourth is a community environmental program that goes beyond compliance. And the fifth is research and evaluation that measures the results of community practice programs.

A company may operate other site community practice programs. Public-private partnerships between the company and a community agency or organization, plant tours, open houses, festivals for children, and sponsorship of charity events are some examples. These are important but not necessary. To be successful in an activist environment, a company's community strategy must contain a minimum of five essential programs.

In this chapter, I will describe three of the essential programs—relationship-building, philanthropy, and community environmental programs. The next chapter will include employee voluntarism, and research and evaluation.

Building Relationships

The aim of the relationship-building programs is to achieve a relationship equal to the third, or escalating, phase of the Bruning–

Ledingham scale of relationships described in chapter 8. There are some shared attitudes, opinions, and interests. There is a great deal of comfort and ease in communication. Trust, respect, and openness are characteristics in this phase. Examples of relationship-building programs used by companies include:

Key contact programs. A fairly common relationship building technique and a way to identify explicit and implicit expectations is a *key contact program.* Key leaders—those identified on the stakeholder relations chart described in chapter 7—are contacted on a periodic basis, commonly once a year or whenever an emergency or change in operations is made. The scope of the discussion is twofold: What, in the opinion of the stakeholder, are the key issues and concerns in the community, and how is the company perceived in the community? By keeping the second question general, that is, not asking for the stakeholder's view but the general community's view, the answer can be steered away from the personal to the general.

The most successful key contact programs are those conducted by general managers rather than community relations managers or consultants. The whole purpose is to form a trust relationship between a manager and a key stakeholder, a relationship in which the manager and the external stakeholder are comfortable with each other. Each has a sense of the other's views on social, economic, political, and cultural issues. There are some shared attitudes, opinions, and interests. There is a great deal of comfort and ease in communication, along with a sense of trust, respect, and openness.

Nongovernmental organization contact programs. A variation of the key contact program is the *NGO contact program.* Companies that are fearful that the individual key contact method may raise expectations or unnecessary questions about the company often rely on information from managers who are volunteers in NGOs. This technique depends on a targeted manager volunteer program.

Management employees are urged to volunteer for an organization selected in consultation with the manager's direct report. One criterion of the selection process is to avoid too many managers volunteering for one organization. The aim is to promote company participation in a broad range of community NGOs. More about this later.

Community Advisory Panels. Companies with sensitive manufacturing processes, such as chemical and oil, depend upon a committee of community representatives known as a *Community Advisory Panel (CAP).* The Chemical Manufacturers Association, the trade association of chemical companies, has been a leading proponent of CAPs.

The association provides technical assistance to companies that want to develop a CAP and is a rich source of information on how CAPs are organized and run.

Community advisory panels serve as a liaison between a company and its communities. They provide a structure for addressing community concerns and questions about a company, and they are a valuable and rich source of information, particularly information about community expectations. Kodak, for example, depends upon CAPs for two reasons: one, to help the company identify the quality of life issues in their community—noise, odors, and the appearance of the company—and, two, to provide a constructive relationship for managing the expectations of residents and local groups.

Another company, Monsanto, relies on CAPs to increase community awareness about the company and to learn about issues concerning the plant. The members of the CAP, which meets quarterly, include the mayor, science teachers, city council members, state extension officers, conservation committee members, and farmers.

There are four types of CAPs. One is an ad hoc panel that is convened as needed by a facility manager to discuss an issue of concern or to advise the company on a specific project—expanding the facility, changing traffic routing patterns, or modifying manufacturing processes, are examples. BC Hydro Company, discussed in chapter 4, used the ad hoc CAP approach.

A second type is a formal CAP organized and supported by the company that meets regularly (usually three to four times a year, although there are some that meet monthly). The panel elects its own chairperson and the company provides staff support and structure.

Where there are a number of companies in a community or area, companies will develop a consortium CAP. This type functions like a company panel, but the companies focus on solving mutual problems or pursuing mutual goals.

Finally, the fourth type is an independent CAP set up by a third party. The League of Women Voters, for example, has been contracted to set up and staff panels as independent contracting consultants for a few companies.

CAPs have also been used to assist a company in planning its philanthropy programs. "The establishment of community advisory panels," said a manager of Reilly Industries, "really caused us to rethink our contributions programs. One result is that monetary and time contributions are being more tightly focused on the community in the immediate vicinity of the plant."[10]

Bristol-Myers Squibb reached out to an ad hoc neighborhood committee, critical of the companies operations, and invited a representative of the committee to serve on its community advisory panel in Syracuse, New York. This provided direct communication between the company and the neighborhood association, allowing it to allay fears, prevent rumors, and address the committee's concerns. The company was able to respond to the concerns (reducing noise, odors, and offensive strobe lights from trucks) quickly and successfully. The committee reported, "Bristol is very open to continue to discuss and assist our neighborhood group. We are very pleased with the process and look forward to a working relationship with our corporate neighbor."[11] This is an excellent example of how to manage the psychological contract.

While CAPs are successful in developing cooperative liaisons with companies, they do involve a considerable investment in time and money. Many companies hire consultants to manage their CAPs. The disadvantage is that the facility managers tend to be removed, although not intentionally, from any interaction among community stakeholders. Relationships, consequently, are made with the consultant and not the company's managers.

The Philanthropy Programs

Corporate philanthropy is perplexing. On the one hand, as I mentioned earlier, very few people are ever aware of what nongovernmental organizations a company supports with its charitable donations. Some 70 percent of residents in Muscatine, Iowa, could not name a single contribution a Monsanto plant had made in the community.[12]

Nonetheless, the public expects companies to be charitable. It is what a company is supposed to do. In fact, often, to the annoyance of community relations managers and foundation executives, charities commonly take what a company gives for granted. The caveat is, as Merck advises in its community relations manual for managers:

> Contributions will not allow a site to buy its way out of a difficult situation. Strategic philanthropy is an important, even laudable, component of "Neighbor of Choice." It is not, however, a substitute for hard work and open communications that build relationships of trust.[13]

Contributions can also be controversial. Antiabortion groups forced AT&T to withdraw its contribution to Planned Parenthood. The Bank of America, Wells Fargo Company, and Levi Strauss were publicly criticized and picketed for cutting off contributions to the Boy Scouts for the Scouts' refusal to admit gays as members or leaders.

What companies have learned from these experiences and findings is that a successful philanthropy program should try to accomplish four tasks:

First, due diligence. A manager should determine that organizations the company is willing to support meet a number of criteria before they are considered for a donation. Some of the questions that should be asked include:

- Does the organization meet legal and statutory requirements to qualify as a not-for-profit organization?
- Does the organization fulfill a genuine community or societal need?
- Is the organization managed according to professional standards, and does it adhere to the operating standards of its profession?
- Does the organization have a leadership structure (volunteer and professional) to carry out the programs that might be supported by the company?
- Does the organization have an active board or committee overseeing the activities of the organization?
- Does the organization publish an annual report, including an audited account of its income and expenses?
- Are there provisions that allow for rotation of board membership?
- Does the organization have the sufficient human and financial resources to carry out its present programs and functions?
- Is the organization respected and trusted by its clients, professional colleagues, key opinion leaders, and other companies in the community?

Second, set priorities. Companies are confronted with requests for contributions from a large number of worthy organizations, far larger than a company can support. It has to make decisions that will disappoint a number of organizations and make a few happy. The manager needs a rationale to explain why the company is giving donations to one organization and not another.

One way companies deal with this is to make a distinction between programs that are of major concern to the company and the community and those that are of secondary or lesser concern to the company and the community. Major programs are often called focused or signature programs. They are generally two or at most three kinds of signature programs a company should support, because experience suggests that spreading small donations among a large number of organizations is not effective in meeting the major needs and concerns of communities.

Nonsignature, or discretionary, programs are often small organizations (libraries, volunteer fire departments, and a recreation park, for example) or donations that are made on a one-time basis (building campaign for community agency and emergency response to a catastrophe). After an analysis by the company (see the following paragraphs) these are programs that do not meet the company's definition of a major focus.

There will also be requests for donations that fall outside the signature and the discretionary programs. Denials to these requests, however, are based on a reasonable answer—the request, it is explained to the organization, falls outside the company's focus for contributions. While disappointed, most NGOs are willing to accept the decision, particularly if, in its letter of denial, the company describes how it went about setting the priorities for contributions.

Selection of signature programs that will receive the major amount of donations to local charities generally is made after making an assessment of community needs and company needs. A community needs assessment can be conducted by the company, in ways discussed earlier. Another source of information on community needs is assessments conducted by other organizations. United Ways local planning agencies of city government, as well as social welfare organizations, often conduct community needs assessments that companies can use as a substitute for conducting their own needs assessment. There is no sense, as many companies say, in repeating what others have done.

Another method for setting contributions priorities is to conduct an internal or company assessment. Companies depend on many services in a community to achieve business goals.

- An educationally prepared workforce;
- A safe and secure environment for employees and their families;
- Day care services for children and adults;
- Recreational and cultural facilities to enhance the quality of life;
- Adequate transportation; and
- A community free of discord and animosity.

When a company focuses its community programs to support its business goals, it is able to exploit its own resources and unique strengths. Moreover, employees are more likely to volunteer in community organizations that enable them to use their knowledge, experience, and skills. The former CEO of IBM, Louis Gerstner, for example, explains that IBM began to treat the recipients of grants as customers and offered them access to the best technology and talent in the company.[14] Everyone benefits.

Another example is Motorola, which focuses its contributions program on education because it is the foundation for promoting economic, social, and technological development around the world. It provides basic equipment and supports many primary, secondary, and university level institutions. It concentrates on programs that enrich experiences in science and math.[15]

These needs can be factored in to the contributions' decision by comparing them with the community needs assessments. Many companies now develop a matrix analysis of company and community needs. Figure 11.1 is an example.[16]

By focusing contributions in the upper right-hand quadrant of the matrix, a company is able to make decisions that reflect both community and company needs. It also is able to present a rationale for its decisions that is sound and defensible.

Another method for determining the major focus for a company's contributions is to survey employees. Employees are an often forgotten but valuable resource in a company's entire citizenship program. When employees are consulted on charitable donations, they feel pleased and honored. They are, after all, one of the major consumers of the services of community organizations. Consequently, they are an excellent source of information about community needs.

A popular philanthropy option that takes into consideration employee needs is a contributions program linked to an employee volunteer program. Known as donor incentive programs, employees are able to request donations, commonly $250 to $1,000, for a community organization in which they serve as volunteers.

Third, build relationships. The two questions a manager should ask when a request is made for a donation are: Will this help us to develop or enhance our relationships with key people in the community? If it does not, how do we design the contributions program so that it does enhance our relationships?

Finally, publicize contributions. At one time, companies rarely publicized their community programs. For some it was inappropriate. But the most common reason for not publicizing donations was the fear

Figure 11.1
Comparison of Community and Company Needs

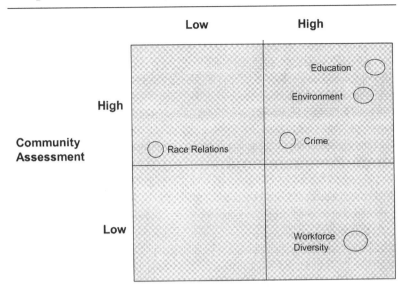

that requests for contributions would increase. The activist society has changed both of these assumptions.

Publicizing community involvement is now the norm. One reason is that studies suggest that a communications strategy that emphasizes the company's philanthropy does improve stakeholder loyalty to a company.[17] But any communications program for philanthropy must be done in context—a context of building trust. The message cannot be self-serving. It has to be informative. Merck puts it this way: "If we don't let our communities know about our integrity and ability, then we haven't allowed them to evaluate our operations. When that happens, we forfeit an opportunity to deepen our relationships of trust."[18]

One other, and frequently neglected, audience for learning about a company's contributions, is employees. Company studies reveal that employees are sadly uninformed about a company's contributions and community programs. Successful companies describe and publicize their community programs on a regular basis with employees. It enhances loyalty to the company. Employees feel proud to be associated with a company that cares to support its needs. It is part of the relationship-building plan.

Environment Programs

The environment is often considered separate from a company's site community programs. It is run by specialists—environmental, health, and safety managers—who are often trained in engineering. But environment has both headquarters or company-wide consequences and community consequences. To consider it separate from a site community strategy is to focus a company's environmental programs on risk management and neglect opportunities to build and foster relationships in communities and nations. It also prevents a company from anticipating issues and concerns.

Environmental management is admittedly a complex task requiring considerable skill and knowledge. Specialists are needed to help a company manage its environmental programs in order to comply with federal and state laws and regulations. But, as I shall explain in the next chapter on societal community strategies, activists are pressing companies to go beyond compliance and to adopt programs of environmental sustainability.

As all facility managers know, they are held responsible for compliance with the Superfund Amendments and Reauthorization Act of 1986 (SARA Title III) and the Community Right to Know legislation. This is a significant responsibility. But facility and general managers as well are accountable to the environmental expectations of all community stakeholders. And it is these stakeholders who are defining the new rules for environmental responsibility.

Some companies are working to develop relationships with environmental stakeholders through the Local Area Planning Committee established as part of the SARA Title III legislation. In Monsanto's plant in Luling, Louisiana, the environmental manager coordinates his work with the company's manager given responsibility for community relations. In one instance, the environmental manager asked for funds from the company's contribution budget to aid the volunteer fire department. Both the community relations manager and the environment, health and safety manager collaborated on the project.

The Abbot Corporation community relations staff works closely with the company's environmental managers. This is an informal relationship.

Thus, environmental management is not only a compliance program but also a part of a community strategy. And when it is part of a community strategy, it changes the mentality of managers. It shifts the orientation of environment away from a strategy of litigation and fighting environmental regulations. If environmental responsibility is seen as part of a community relationship-building strategy, then the focus of attention is on becoming sensitive to community environmental expectations.

Equally important, it focuses management attention on emerging and shifting expectations about environmental performance of the company and its industry. It is an anticipatory and opportunistic plan. Managers are able to develop responses to the shifts, opening the opportunity to negotiate changes. The management of the company becomes part of the decision-making process and thus better able to work out compromises.

Consequently, it promotes the competitive advantage of the company. As Harvard Business School professor Michael Porter and Claas Van Der Linde of Switzerland's Institute for International Management Research learned, "Businesses spend too many of their environmental dollars on fighting regulation and not enough on finding real solutions." A Rand Institute for Civil Justice discovered that 88 percent of the money that insurers paid out between 1986 and 1989 on Superfund claims went to pay for legal and administrative costs. Only 12 percent was used for the actual clean up of sites.[19]

Companies that integrate their environmental efforts and programs with their site community strategies discover significant benefits. For years, the Polaroid Corporation, for example, was listed in the Boston press as a leading polluter in Massachusetts. Yet, it was not criticized by environmentalists. The company had built up a positive relationship in its highly praised community strategies and, as a result, environmentalists gave the company the benefit of the doubt when the company said it was working on efforts to reduce pollution in the manufacturing processes.

SUMMARY

A site community strategy is a requirement for maintaining a company's license to operate. Three of the five essential elements of a site community strategy have been described in this chapter.

CHAPTER 12

The Site Community Strategy, Continued

E mployee voluntarism: A win for the community and a win for the company.

That boast is repeated often by community relations managers as a way to sell employee volunteer programs in a company. And there is a great deal of truth to the statement, so much so that it deserves separate and special treatment. There is little doubt that communities and companies benefit from employee volunteer programs. That alone accounts for the tremendous increase in corporate employee volunteer programs.

The number of companies assisting employees with volunteer efforts is increasing about 25 percent a year, according to Hewitt Associates, a human resources consulting firm. The vast majority of companies selected in surveys of the best companies to work for have organized employee volunteer programs. In 1990, fewer than 20 percent of major companies listed employee voluntarism as part of their business plant. By 1999, the figure was 48 percent.

But what about the employees? Do they benefit? Is it also a win for them? Let us see.

THE WIN FOR THE COMPANY

There is convincing evidence that a company's volunteer program can provide considerable benefits for a company. One reason is that a well-run volunteer program helps to promote the company's citizenship reputation. This in turn assists the company in recruiting and retaining employees.[1] In a period in which employees are viewed as the investment capital of the twenty-first century, this is a significant and important finding.

Skill development. Employee volunteer programs have been found to be a superb professional development tool. Companies are using volunteer programs to teach employees new skills, upgrade existing skills, and provide opportunities for employees to test new skills in real-life situations. Thom McCann and United Parcel Service (UPS), for example, have used volunteer programs to help managers become sensitive to diversity issues.[2] General Electric uses its volunteer programs to teach team-building skills.[3]

Peter Drucker, the widely respected consultant and expert on management, calls volunteering for nonprofit organizations "perhaps the best educational experience I could advise for a thirty-five-year-old manager."[4]

Research by a few companies like Pillsbury has discovered more than twenty-five skills employees can learn in a volunteer experience. These include:

Assertiveness
Budget management
Change management
Communication skills
Computer skills
Cultural awareness
Interpersonal skills
Leadership
Listening skills
Managing people
Motivating others
Needs analysis
Negotiating skills
Planning skills
Presentation skills
Risk-taking
Time management

Pillsbury pioneered in designing questionnaires that can be used by employees to select a volunteer program or activity that can provide a learning experience in improving skill areas called "Development Through Volunteerism," and "Development Opportunities: Management and Supervisory Skills."[5] (See Chart 12.1 and 12.2 at the end of the chapter.) The questionnaires have been duplicated by many other companies.

The Development Opportunities chart can be used in two ways. Employees on their own initiative select areas they would like to develop and seek out agencies that can provide the practices that improve the skill. They also can fill out a questionnaire and submit it to the director of the Pillsbury Employee Volunteer Program.

A manager can also use the Development Opportunities chart in a regularly scheduled supervisory session to guide an employee in identifying skills that need to be improved and then help the employee locate an agency that can offer the practice experience needed to improve the skill.

Building positive relationships through voluntarism. Another benefit to a company of an employee volunteer program is that it can be a useful tool for enhancing its image among key stakeholders. Community surveys, some going as far back as the 1950s, consistently report that residents who know an employee are more favorable to the company than those who have no relationship with an employee. That is a significant finding. An Opinion Research Corporation study in 1955 discovered that community attitudes about companies are obtained chiefly from "someone I know who works there."[6]

Another way of stating it is that employees are ambassadors of a company. They promote favorability. Consequently, the more the company promotes voluntarism, the more it is likely to improve its relationships with stakeholders and, therefore, its reputation in the community. Similar to the professional development advantages of employee voluntarism, the benefits to the company far exceed the costs.

Employee voluntarism programs have also been found to increase loyalty to a company. Companies, according to Robert Goodwin, president of the Points of Light Foundation, an organization that studies and promotes voluntarism, are finding that an employee volunteer program can aid in attracting and retaining skilled employees.

As a consequence of these benefits, many companies are targeting their employee volunteer programs. The community affairs staff prepares material and facilitates the development of volunteer opportunities. Managers, however, are responsible for implementing the programs.

It should begin with a targeted goal. Frequently, it is stated as

improve and strengthen the company's relationships with key stakeholders in the community through a targeted employee voluntarism program.

Note: the goal is not just to influence the relationship. It is a two-way relationship. Building trust relationships means that a company has to be open to listening and responding to the concerns and shifting expectations of the community stakeholders. The emphasis is on developing and maintaining workable trust relationships.

Managers meet with selected exempt employees to assess the range and scope of their volunteer activities. The objective is to spread the base of participation in community agencies and minimize the chances that a majority of employees are serving in volunteer activities of one or two agencies in the community.

CREATING INCENTIVES FOR INCREASING VOLUNTARISM IN THE COMPANY

From 1997 to 2001, companies with employee volunteer programs increased from 70 percent to 83 percent, according to the annual Center for Corporate Citizenship surveys. Despite the increase in employee voluntarism, community relations managers say that convincing employees to become volunteers cannot be taken for granted. At the International Corporate Citizenship Conference of the Center for Corporate Citizenship in San Francisco in March 2004, many community relations managers reported that it was becoming increasingly difficult to persuade employees to volunteer in community organizations.

Some reasons offered were that employees feel too stressed to find time to volunteer. Others reported that employees believed they are not rewarded for employee volunteer projects. What employees do on a volunteer project for a company is taken for granted. And still others commented that the Enron, MCI, and Tyco scandals soured the relationship between companies and employees. Employees would much prefer to volunteer for projects that are not sponsored by a company.

Generating incentives to encourage and increase employee voluntarism is becoming ever more critical. One technique is to highlight and publicize the volunteer activities of company leaders, like the CEO. Studies show that when employees know that the leadership is involved in the community, morale and loyalty to the company increases and it becomes much easier to sell the employees on the value of volunteering in community programs.

Another technique is to design a donor incentive program such as those briefly described in the previous chapter. J. P. Morgan Chase bank, for example, donates $1,000 in the name of an individual volunteer and $2,000 for team projects to a nonprofit organization. The company also donates $3,000 to the agency of choice to honor the company's chosen volunteer of the year.

A third method is recognition and reward programs. To promote volunteers in the Boston public schools, the John Hancock Insurance Company ran full-page ads in the newspaper listing every employee who volunteered. The ad was headlined with the phrase: "If you think this list is long, you should see the names of the kids they helped." At the end of the school year, the company held a ceremony involving the mayor, volunteers, and students.

Annual awards ceremonies are common because companies combine programs that not only honor volunteers but also showcase the company's corporate citizenship. Freeport-MacMoRan of New Orleans, for example, invites representatives of the community's charitable organization to its annual volunteer awards program. The CEO thanks the volunteers and the agencies.

In Orange County, California, the Volunteer Action Center, a non-profit organization, coordinates and conducts an annual recognition program. Nonprofit organizations submit the names of corporate volunteers they want to be recognized as "outstanding volunteers." Some 700 volunteers are hosted at a Disney Hotel in what is described in Orange County as the "Oscars" of volunteer awards.

Released-time programs are also becoming increasingly popular. Some are informal. Genzyme, the biotech company, allows employees to make informal arrangements with their managers when they will be engaged in volunteer work during business hours. J. P. Morgan Chase community relations staff works with managers to determine when employees can volunteer.

A growing number of companies are developing released-time policies. AT&T allows employees one day annually to volunteer on an individual project or as part of a team. Ford Motor Company permits salaried employees to volunteer sixteen hours annually when they are part of a team of five or more employees on projects linked to Ford contributions.

A WIN FOR THE COMMUNITY

The question of whether employee voluntarism is a win for the site community has never truly been answered. It is assumed.

The growth of employee voluntarism was born of necessity. Charitable and government agencies began to besiege corporations for donations in the late 1980s and early 1990s. Faced with decreases in federal and state support, corporations looked to businesses for an answer. In fact, as I noted earlier, they were encouraged to do so by newly elected President Ronald Reagan who, in a speech to the National Alliance for Business, asked corporations to increase their financial support of local charities.

As a consequence, corporate contributions soared. Between 1976 and 1985, corporate donations to charities tripled, rising from $1.5 to $4.4 billion. But corporations did not sustain that rate of increase. Since 1980, corporate contributions increased but at significantly reduced rates. In some years, the increase did not keep pace with inflation.

Nonetheless, the local charities, which had increased in number during that period, continued to grow. In addition, tax-supported agencies—schools, mental health services, highway departments, and juvenile delinquency organizations—joined in the request for corporate dollars. This was an entirely new "market" asking for help.

Corporations turned to the employee volunteer technique for providing some measure of support to charities. The NGOs, however, preferred cash. Managing volunteers became an added—and unplanned—task. But corporations were unwilling to increase their contribution budgets. Employee voluntarism for the NGOs became the tactic of choice.

In some cases, they have been oversold. Social problems are long-standing and deep-seated. Children in the inner city have to struggle with poor schools, lack of decent medical care, single- or no-parent households, racism, drugs, and few healthy role models. It is difficult for employee volunteer programs to meet these needs, however well intentioned.

True, studies do show that mentoring does reduce drop out rates and drug use among teenagers. But for that kind of mentoring to be successful, it has to be long term and consistent. Youngsters depend on their mentors. Faced with rejection from parents, school, and friends, they rely on the mentor for long-term emotional support, a type of support that many employees find it difficult to sustain, or even offer.

Most employees prefer volunteering for projects that are time limited. They also find it difficult to leave their families in the suburbs and travel to the inner city to carry out such volunteer assignments.

On the whole, there is little evidence that employee voluntarism programs are effective. There are too few studies on the efficacy and effectiveness of employee voluntarism programs. The little evidence that employee voluntarism is a win for the community is anecdotal.

A WIN FOR THE EMPLOYEE?

The real winners of the employee voluntarism programs, it is fairly obvious, are companies. In fact, a focused and organized employee volunteer program is obviously an impressive cost saver. In fact, there is nothing a company does to enhance its corporate citizenship or to enhance its relationships—community relations, public affairs, lobbying, publicity—that can provide as many benefits as a well-managed and targeted employee voluntarism program. Nothing!

The trend in Europe is to exploit employee voluntarism programs, use them for competitive advantage. Companies in Europe are developing loaned executive programs (called secondments in the United Kingdom). Some are of long duration—three to six months. Others are on a day-a-week basis for a period of three to six months.

Loaned executive programs in the United States have failed to catch on because they have a poor reputation. Introduced by United Way in the 1950s, they were hailed as a way to increase volunteer help for the United Way during its annual campaign and as a management training tool. Loaned executives were promised that they would learn public speaking and planning skills over a three-month period.

Those selected, however, were dispensable or soon to be dispensable. Few executives, consequently, volunteer to be loaned executives. Those asked to be loaned executives frequently looked for excuses to refuse the request.

Xerox and IBM companies had what were called sabbatical programs. Managers could request a sabbatical to work for an NGO for up to twelve months. Managers liked these programs. Downsizing and the increasing competitiveness of the global economy made these programs a luxury difficult to sustain.

Why not pay employees for volunteering? If companies benefit overwhelmingly from volunteer programs, why shouldn't employees also benefit? They should be financially compensated. Offering employees one day off a year or a month does not compensate employees. Management employees still have to make up for the time they take off. Projects are not cut back. Additional support to assist a manager engaged in a volunteer program is not offered. These incentives are not compensation.

But is paying employees engaged in volunteer work, even if it is for the company's benefit, true voluntarism? That is the frequent cry of critics for a compensated volunteer program. Yet, many people engage in volunteer activities, not just for the intrinsic value of voluntarism but for secondary gains. It is a way, for example, to advance within the company by improving skills. It can be an opportunity, too, to meet managers in other parts of the company. And for many, it is a socializing opportunity. Walkathons for charities are popular for the twenty-something employee precisely because it is a way to meet people.

Because people have different motives for volunteering does not devalue the volunteer activity. In fact, just the opposite is true. The more a person benefits from a volunteer activity, the more likely he or she will be committed to the project and the nongovernmental organization.

One answer to those who are uncomfortable with paying employees for volunteer work is to change the name. Call them "Employee Involvement" programs. If they qualify, an employee can choose to be part of the company's employee involvement program or decide to work as a volunteer in an organization without compensation.

A radical suggestion? Possibly. But companies spend huge sums of money to improve their institutional image, foster relationships with government officials, or maintain their license to operate. Employee volunteer programs, managed effectively, can achieve all these objectives more easily and less expensively—and improve employee skills and morale at the same time. What other external program can make this boast?

RESEARCH AND MEASUREMENT

The one weakness in the development of community strategies has been the absence of efforts to measure results. A number of studies have been conducted to demonstrate the value, or the business case, of corporate citizenship. But these were motivated by a young and emerging "profession" of corporate community relations managers to challenge the criticism that community relations were cost centers.

Once the business case was made, efforts to evaluate performance began to gain speed. Often, it was spearheaded by senior executives in companies. Lou Gerstner, IBM CEO, for example, challenged companies to run corporate citizenship like any other business opportunity. "How do we ensure," he said, "that we are measuring results not just activity?

"In no other area of corporate endeavor," he continued "—not in advertising, not in research, and certainly not in marketing or manufacturing—would we evaluate our effectiveness simply by measuring how much we spend. Why should philanthropy be unique?"[7]

Gerstner's message is getting attention. Research and evaluation is becoming part of a community strategy's planning process. But research and evaluation appear to be carried out at two levels. One is at the community level.

One type of evaluation is determining that a contribution was used as the nonprofit organization claimed it would be. There have been cases of fraud on the part of nonprofit organizations, some of which were widely reported in the press.

The lesson is, at the very least, general managers should conduct a simple audit of contributions to local charities. It is a due-diligence issue. Did the funds given by the company go to the program they were intended to go to? Were they used as the agency said they would be?

Another technique for auditing contributions is to "assign" employees to serve on the board or committee of a community organization to provide oversight and consulting functions in addition to the volunteer duties. In fact, this service often can be more valuable than donating money. Research and evaluation skills are in short supply in most NGOs. Providing this service can be a valuable contribution to charitable organizations.

Answering questions of results or accomplishments is much harder. Social service organizations request donations to solve many serious, almost intractable, programs—juvenile delinquency, child and spouse abuse, teenage pregnancies, illiteracy, increasing math skills, and upgrading public education, to cite a few examples. Solutions come slowly if at all. But here, too, companies can provide a consultation and mentoring skill that may be equally as valuable as a financial contribution.

Another obstacle is the imprecision of terms. This is a problem raised by academic researchers. Academics have had difficulty measuring corporate citizenship because of the disagreement over the term as a theoretical construct.[8]

At the local community level, companies can make a significant contribution by donating research staff to assist nonprofit organizations in improving their research activities. IBM has made helping community level organizations improve their technical capacities as part of its ambitious new strategy called "IBM On Demand Community," that will be described in the next chapter.

At the corporate level, corporations are beginning to expand their institutional and brand reputation studies to include "community reputation." Former NYU business school professor and expert on reputation analysis C. J. Fombrun[9] is working with a number of companies, including Bristol-Myers Squibb, helping them to design and carryout community reputation studies.

Another area of research needed is a study of a company's level of relationships with key external stakeholders. The Bruning–Ledingham scale described in chapter 8 is a useful format for developing ways to evaluate relationships with stakeholders.

THE COMMUNITY RELATIONS MANAGERS' RESPONSIBILITIES

If, as I argued at the outset, the site manager has to be held accountable for the behavior and reputation of the company in a site community, what happens to the role of the community relations manager?

It has slowly been changing from being a doer to that of a facilitator and analyst. Prior to the 1990s, community relations was primarily a part-time function. Only 9 percent of community relations managers were full-time, according to a survey conducted by The Center for Corporate Community Relations in 1987.[10]

Further, those engaged in community relations—part-time and full-time—had moved into the field from other administrative staff positions within the company or from management positions in public relations, communications, or public affairs. The function of the community relations manager was often to organize and run the United Way drive, attend community functions on behalf of the company, and orchestrate the public presentations of the site manager and the CEO.

Ten years later, a remarkable change had taken place. Over 75 percent of the respondents to a similar Center study conducted in 1997 reported that they were engaged full time in "doing" community relations. Today, that is closer to 100 percent. Moreover, the tasks of community relations were greatly expanded. Community relations professionals engaged in strategic external affairs functions for the corporation, including relationship building and issues management. Some 25 percent reported that community relations were organized as a separate function, an increase from 18 percent four years earlier in 1993.

But in the era of corporate citizenship, the role of community relations managers is changing. This is not uncharacteristic in management. Any new management, explains Michael Porter, goes through a predictable life cycle. At first companies hire outside experts. Once the practice becomes fully developed it is turned over to internal specialists, in our case the community relations manager. After the field becomes mature companies begin to integrate it into the ongoing role of line management. That is precisely what is happening at the moment.[11]

Community relations managers are becoming less the "doers" of corporate citizenship and more the facilitators of the practice. They are becoming coaches for general managers, aiding them to carry out corporate citizenship responsibilities in site communities.

They facilitate the work of the site and general managers in setting strategies, designing plans, and preparing them for public presentations in site communities. They are also becoming the specialists in research and evaluation. They provide the analytical tools to assist general managers and site managers in carrying out their corporate citizenship responsibilities.

SUMMARY

Setting strategies, developing plans, and managing the external relations of the company in site communities is the role of the site community manager. In this chapter, techniques for carrying out this emerging and heavy responsibility have been described.

Chart 12.1
Employee Development Worksheet Used by Pillsbury Corporation

DEVELOPMENT THROUGH VOLUNTEERISM
Employee Development Worksheet

Name: _____   Department: _____

Title: _____   Date: _____

The purpose of this worksheet is to help you identify areas where you could benefit from developmental opportunities through volunteerism. You and your supervisor can use this information to create a developmental plan or refer to your own developmental plan. Your plan may include such things as training courses, on-the-job assignments or cross-training opportunities. Other developmental opportunities exist through volunteer services with a variety of community organizations.

What do you see as your talents that help you do your job well? _____

_____

What types of tasks best utilize these talents? _____

_____

What do you see as your greatest developmental needs? _____

_____

Is there any area where you think you need additional technical or skill training? _____

_____

List any types of volunteer projects that you would be interested in doing to meet your developmental goals. _____

_____

Chart 12.2
Development Opportunities: Management and Supervisory Skills

Skill/Development Area	Ways to Practice
Budget Management	Chair a finance committee Plan an events budget Chair an event with a budget Volunteer for a board position with finance responsibilities Plan promotions on a budget
Change Management/ Strategic Awareness	Help with group bylaws Participate on an organization board Serve on personnel committee Do strategic planning for an organization Help write vision statement for an organization Participate in a focus group Write/rewrite job descriptions Be an active participant in a changing organization
Leadership	Serve as the chair of a committee Supervise volunteers Be the spokesperson for a group or organization Work with young people as a tutor/mentor
Managing People	Manage volunteers Coordinate an event Volunteer to be a facilitator
Develop/Motivating Others	Be a tutor/mentor Work in a fund-raising activity Chair a committee Be a United Way team captain Promote an event or organization
Problem Solving and Decision Making	Answer calls for a hot line Volunteer as a counselor Serve as a mentor/tutor Plan an event Work on a construction project

(*continued*)

Chart 12.2 Continued

Skill/Development Area	Ways to Practice
Computer Skills	Develop a database Utilize a new word processing program Apply systems applications on a database
Needs Analysis	Develop a strategic plan Volunteer at a school Develop surveys Organize the acquisition and distribution of resources Serve on a finance committee Volunteer as a counselor
Organizational Skills	Plan an event Edit a newsletter Provide clerical services Coordinate a multisponsored event
Planning	Plan an event Help produce a newsletter Serve on a strategic planning committee Coordinate an event or activity
Project Management	Plan an event Be a tutor/mentor Edit a newsletter Coordinate/monitor an ongoing project
Facilitation	Lead a committee meeting Conduct a class Coordinate a group process
Listening Skills	Volunteer to answer calls for a hot line Serve as a tutor/mentor Provide crisis intervention counseling Work with sick people
Presentation Skills	Become part of a speaker's bureau Serve as a team captain for United Way Do public relations work Be a spokesperson Be the master of ceremonies for an event

Chart 12.2 Continued

Skill/Development Area	Ways to Practice
Verbal Communication	See Presentation Skills above
Written Communication	Write for a newsletter Develop letters for fund-raising Take minutes at meetings Write grant proposals Serve as the secretary for a group, organization, or event
Assertiveness	Serve as a fundraiser, solicit pledges or support Participate in a registration drive Be a recruiter

Conflict Resolution/
    Negotiation
	Serve on a board
	Negotiate contracts or personnel issues
	Manage a function or event
	Participate in the planning/execution of
	    multicommittee events

Cultural Awareness	Volunteer in an activity that works close with people unlike yourself Be a tutor/mentor Make presentations to diverse audiences Serve on a public relations committee
Flexibility/Resiliency	Volunteer with children, the elderly, or persons with disabilities Volunteer in a crisis center Coordinate other volunteers Work on an outdoor event

Interpersonal skills	Assume a leadership role in an activity
	    that involves a group of people
	Become part of a speaker's bureau
	Do the public relations work for an event
	    or organization
	Recruit volunteers
	Do fund-raising
	Volunteer to answer calls for a hot line
	Be a tutor/mentor

(*continued*)

Chart 12.2 Continued

Skill/Development Area	Ways to Practice
Networking	Edit a newsletter Do public relations work Acquire resources Conduct surveys Solicit funds or participation Recruit volunteers or members Serve on a board
Reliability/Follow-up	Voter registration Coordinate an adopt-a-family project Be a mentor/tutor
Risk-taking	Coordinate volunteers Get involved with a new activity Participate in the start-up of a new organization or event Plan an outdoor activity or event
Selling	Assist with fund-raising Recruit volunteers Serve as an organization sponsor/liaison
Taking Initiative	Serve as a fundraiser Participate in the start-up of a new organization or event Recruit volunteers Solicit resources
Teamwork	Work on a construction or rehab project Be a coach Collaborate with others on a project Plan/coordinate an event Serve on a board
Time Management Prioritizing	Volunteer at a school Manage resources, facilitate meetings

CHAPTER 13

The Societal Strategy—
The CEO's Responsibility

In the early morning hours of Saturday, September 29, 1997, an eighteen-year-old MIT freshman, Scott Krueger, was rushed from a fraternity house to the Beth Israel Deaconess Medical Center in a coma after a night of binge drinking that was part of a fraternity initiation program. The level of alcohol in Krueger's body was .410, five times the legal limit for a driver in Massachusetts. He never came out of the coma.

Krueger's death from binge drinking was not an isolated event. Three other college students died from binge drinking in the same year. Beer drinking by underage students was a weekly event and appeared to be a college rite of passage.

According to nationwide survey in 1995, two years before Krueger's death, 44 percent of college students admitted to binge drinking. Over 85 percent of fraternity members and 80 percent of sorority members admitted to binge drinking weekly.

Krueger's parents were devastated and angry. They accused MIT of neglecting its responsibility to young students under its charge. Given the widespread knowledge of underage drinking, MIT should have established policies and procedures that could have prevented the death of their son. MIT was complicit in their son's death by tacitly encouraging a culture that tolerated alcohol abuse by students. They brought suit against the university.

September 13, 2000, three years after Krueger's death, an agreement was reached between MIT and the Kruegers. MIT agreed to contribute $1.25 million for scholarships to be established by the Kruegers and, in addition, paid them $4.75 million.

The national publicity given to the death of Scott Krueger, along with the financial award to the Krueger family, spurred colleges into action. MIT made major changes in its policies. It required all first-year students to live on campus and not in fraternity or sorority houses. Fraternities and sororities were required to have resident advisors. Five fraternities voluntarily declared themselves to be alcohol-free.

MIT set up a comprehensive program to provide treatment and prevention for students and staff. It instituted sanctions for alcohol violations and provided a campuswide and ongoing training program on the use and misuse of alcohol.

Colleges around the country followed MIT's example. Alcohol drinking was found to be the leading cause of campus crime and health problems, claimed administrators. Coming under specific criticism was the alcohol beverage industry, particularly the beer industry because of its promotion of beer drinking in colleges and universities. College administrators were particularly critical, claiming that all their prevention programs were undermined by slick and sophisticated advertisements showing college-age youngsters enjoying alcohol. The industry spent over $50 million in 2002 on commercials televised during college sports programs, according to The Center on Alcohol Marketing and Youth at Georgetown University in Washington, D.C. NCAA tournament games led all other sports events in alcohol-related TV advertising in 2002. There were over 939 ads broadcasted compared with 925 ads run during the Super Bowl, World Series, college bowl games, and "Monday Night Football."[1]

High school administrators chipped in as well. Drinking by teenagers was growing astronomically. The *Washington Post* reported that 20 percent of eighth grade students had drunk alcohol in the previous thirty days. Forty-nine percent of high school seniors are drinkers, and 29 percent of seniors said that they had five or more drinks in a row in the previous two weeks.[2]

Fear of increased regulations and possible prohibitions against drinking any kind of alcoholic beverage forced the alcohol beverage industry, and beer companies in particular, to reassess their marketing strategies. They did not want to repeat the mistakes of the cigarette industry and be accused of developing a beer-drinking image of Joe Camel.

The industry realized, too, that it could not rely on its community strategies. While community strategies were effective in countering issues similar to the boycott threat against Anheuser-Busch by Rev.

Jesse Jackson, it could not respond to the accusations that its advertising strategies were encouraging binge drinking. It was not just that it was a different issue from the boycott issue. It was because there were different stakeholders, stakeholders who were widely dispersed among many different communities, and who had concerns and issues that went beyond a company's community license to operate. In many of these communities, the company may not even have a physical presence. It was a public issue.

And the public was not looking for relationships, volunteers, or donations. They wanted beer companies to stop underage drinking.

Under threats of suits and growing outrage, beer companies, reluctantly at first, began responding to the public's concerns. They restricted advertisements targeting underage audiences and depicting underage look-alike models in their television and magazine advertising.

They initiated programs that promote responsible drinking at college campuses. They provided colleges with programs that promoted adult drinking on campuses, and they encouraged bars and restaurants to institute procedures to check identification of patrons. They encouraged parents to engage their children in discussions about alcohol and alcohol abuse.

Anheuser-Busch, for example, has initiated a prevention program called "Family Talk." The program asks parents to engage in open, honest communication between themselves and children. It was developed by an advisory panel of education, family counseling, child psychology, and alcohol treatment professionals. A program guide is distributed free to parents and educators by Anheuser-Busch through its national network of distributors. It can also be obtained from the company's Web site. Since 1990, more than five million copies of program materials have been distributed.

The binge-drinking strategies of companies like Anheuser-Busch address concerns of stakeholders beyond the community level where the company may have operating facilities. They are societal and in some cases global in scope. They may in fact target global stakeholders. They respond to specific social issue challenges presented by shifts in social attitudes. Called societal strategies, they are managed at a company's headquarters level. Frequently, they are spearheaded by the CEO, because they are public positioning strategies aimed at preserving and enhancing the company's brand reputation among a wide network of stakeholders, including customers, shareholders, employees, vendors, government officials and regulators, and the general public. Here are some examples.

IBM'S EDUCATION STRATEGY

When Louis Gerstner was appointed CEO of IBM, his first task was to rescue a giant icon of a company that was experiencing meltdown. It was, in Gerstner's own words, "bleeding financially." Profits were sinking substantially. His first job, he declared, was to restore confidence in the company and its products.

Once he was confident he had a handle on IBM's problems, he turned his attention to the company's community involvement programs. At one time, IBM was the world's leader in corporate contributions. Ten years prior to Gerstner joining IBM, the company had contributed annually $1.3 billion to a number of charities, local and national.

Gerstner wanted to focus and prioritize the company's programs. Public education was his primary concern. Education was important because the company depended upon a skilled workforce, and a public education strategy would address an issue that was also a concern of the public.

Education was also Gerstner's long-term passion. Gerstner believed that public education was not keeping up with the emerging needs of a technological society. It was fast becoming irrelevant to the knowledge age. And he also believed that the public wanted great companies to help solve the public education crisis. Public education was a challenge and an opportunity for IBM.

The business community, claimed Gerstner, was in a position to help solve these problems. "Corporations," he said, "as distinct organization in our society, do certain things better than all the other parts of our society. Most important, they know how to plan, manage resources, communicate to constituencies, and conduct many other productive activities that are required by nearly all nonprofit organizations. Skills in these areas are very important for charitable organizations, but such skills are rarely found in sufficient quantities to allow the emergence of successful, self-renewing organizations."[3]

Joining with representatives of the National Governors Association, he initiated annual education summits composed of leaders in business, government (state and federal), and education. The purpose was to rally around an initiative to reform education.

He brought on to the staff an expert in public education from the New York City school system, Stanley Litow, to head up the community relations program. Litow persuaded other experienced educators in the New York school system to join him.

Litow, now IBM vice president of community relations, surveyed key community stakeholders to assess community priorities. Employees were also surveyed to determine what they believed to be the key community issues. Both surveys revealed that improving educations was the top concern, which fit in squarely with Gerstner's assessment.

The company subsequently launched an initiative called "Reinventing Education," which received favorable press notice and developed strong linkages between the company and the nation's school leaders. The company brought teachers, administrators, and even schoolchildren to IBM's laboratories. They worked on eliminating the toughest barriers between children and a world-class education. By the year 2000, more than ten million children and 65,000 teachers were reached through the efforts of IBM researchers and employees. It was a strategy that would address a public and national concern.

Under Gerstner's successor, Sam Palmisano, IBM's education initiative has expanded beyond the initial goals of reforming education. Now called "IBM On Demand Community," the initiative emphasizes employee voluntarism by using the strengths and skills of its employees to provide innovation, new technologies, and solutions to nonprofit organizations. The company aims to use its technological resources to provide significant and measurable change in agencies and organizations.

IBM has developed a unique intranet site that allows employees to identify volunteer opportunities, receive on-line training, and learn technology solutions that can be used by nonprofit organizations. The site lists activities that help promote math and science, and e-mentoring that creates positive change in schools. The program also provides technology planning and assistance for community agencies needing technical and business expertise. In addition, through the intranet site, an employee or retiree volunteer can request grants of IBM equipment and technology discounts for nonprofit agencies and schools.

The strategy is combined with its community strategies and programs which is spearheaded by Ann Cramer, Director of Community Relations for IBM. Cramer calls it part of IBM's "glocalization" emphasis. It is, in effect, a joint strategy combining societal efforts and community programs. What started out as a headquarters-focused strategy to improve and reform education is now a corporate-directed effort that enables IBM volunteers to share the company's strengths with schools and not-for-profit organizations.

Gerstner's reinventing education program made a significant contribution to focusing the attention of the business community on developing solutions for public education. It was a global strategy not restricted to communities in which the company had facilities. More important, Gerstner was able to institutionalize corporate citizenship in a way that has made it become an integral part of the company's vision of what the company should do for society. It is no longer a Gerstner program but an IBM program that could be picked up by his successor, updated, and modernized to use all the technological skills of a great company.

CAUSE MARKETING

In 1983, American Express announced it would donate a penny every time its card was used in a sale, a dollar for each new card issued, and a dollar for every travel package over $500 over a four-month period to the restoration campaign of the Statue of Liberty. Over $1.7 million was raised for the Statue of Liberty project, exceeding all expectations.

The company's results were just as spectacular. Card usage rose 28 percent in one month compared with a similar month the previous year. New card applications increased by 45 percent. American Express caught the wave of changing public expectations toward companies and their support of charities.[4]

News of American Express's success quickly spread among other consumer companies. The benefits of cause-related marketing seemed endless. One study reported that cause-related marketing could help:

Promote a national visibility;
Enhance a corporate image;
Thwart negative publicity;
Generate incremental sales;
Promote repeat purchases;
Promote multiple-unit purchases;
Increase brand awareness;
Reinforce brand image;
Broaden the customer base; and
Reach new market segments.[5]

Another set of researchers writing in 1991 called cause marketing "the most creative and cost-effective product marketing strategy to evolve in years."[6]

A study conducted by Sue Adkins, under the auspices of Business in the Community, provides a number of examples of corporate cause-marketing efforts. Among those described are two of the most well known—Target Stores and Avon.[7]

The Target Company. Target's cause marketing grew out of its concern that its charitable-giving programs received scant attention in the press. It had a long tradition of giving, but it went largely unnoticed, according to Bob Thacker, former senior vice president for marketing. Competitors gave far less to charity than Target Stores, yet they were given more credit.

Cause marketing was viewed as a way to remedy that perception. At the same time, it was an opportunity to differentiate itself among its competitors and reinforce its brand proposition: Expect more, pay less.[8] The cause-marketing program began in the early 1990s.

The initial strategy was to identify a charitable organization and then look for vendors as partners. The company, for example, paired baby products with campaigns against child abuse, crayons and paper with education, and publishers with reading and literacy. Subsequently, Target developed programs that would leverage the company's brand image. They partnered, for example, pharmaceutical and health companies with a campaign to support St. Jude Hospital, a nationally known children's cancer and research hospital. The aim was to increase the awareness of the pharmacies and health and beauty departments in Target stores. Pharmaceutical vendors promised that a percentage of all sales in the pharmacies and the health and beauty department would be contributed to the hospital.

Brochures and campaign literature for St. Jude Hospital were distributed in Target stores. The company also involved celebrities, such as TV and movie star Marlo Thomas and skater Scott Hamilton, to promote the cause-marketing program. This campaign gave Target stores widespread publicity and an increase in sales for pharmaceutical, beauty, and health products.[9]

Avon. Avon Company's cause-marketing program was developed to rescue a company losing markets because of changing demographics. Founded in 1886, Avon became the world's leading direct seller of hair and beauty-related products door to door. Its products were sold in more than 135 countries through independent sales representatives known as the Avon Ladies, using the cheerful slogan "Avon Calling."

In the 1970s and 1980s, however, the work habits of women changed. They began entering the labor market in increasing numbers, taking jobs in business and the professions. Few women were willing to sell the Avon products door to door. Fewer still were home to answer the door to the Avon ladies.

After a series of studies, the company modified its vision, claiming that it would be the company that best understands ands satisfies the product, service, and self-fulfillment needs of women worldwide. It also committed itself to renew its long-term tradition of giving back to the citizens who support it. A survey of its customer base and sales representatives revealed that breast cancer was the overwhelming concern of women.

In 1993, the company launched The Breast Cancer Awareness Crusade in the United Kingdom and the United States. The company initiated support of NGOs that provide early screening and breast cancer awareness programs. It currently partners with the Nation Alliance of Breast Cancer Organizations, the U.S. National Institutes of Health, and the U.S. Centers for Disease Control.

It developed special events programs—walk-a-thons, road races, and early breast cancer fairs—to inform women of the importance of preventing deaths through early detection. It inaugurated a pink ribbon fund-raising campaign that sold pink ribbon pins for two dollars. In three months in 1993, Avon raised more than $5.7 million for cancer agencies.

Avon became known as the company that cared about women and cared enough to do something about it. It received awards worldwide for its breast cancer programs, particularly programs that emphasized early detection. Cone Public Affairs found that, in a study of breast cancer awareness, Avon was first in women knowing about breast cancer programs.

Avon has also become an advocate of cause-related marketing. "The success of Avon's twenty-eight international cause-marketing programmes and the Avon Worldwide Fund for Women's Health," says Joanne Mazurki, Avon's Director of Global Cause Related Marketing, "is the direct result of leveraging our unique strengths as a company. . . . No other company could have delivered the magnitude of support for women's health that Avon has because no other company has our particular resources. Because we have focused what is unique about us, our key constituents—consumers, not-for-profit partners, the government and the media—trust that our efforts have integrity and commitment. Other companies interested in cause marketing should leverage what is unique about their ways of doing business."[10]

SOCIAL ISSUES STRATEGIES

Social issues are a reflection of people's concerns. The noise, pollution, and traffic that a company can cause in its day-to-day operations is an example. Most of these issues are resolved with little difficulty, primarily because of the experience learned in the development of community strategies.

Others, however, can and do balloon out of control. Environmental issues are classic examples. Environmental issues reflect people's worries about the quality of their life. People want to live in communities that are free of environmental risks. The risks may be unfounded and unscientific, but, nonetheless, they can be real to people.

In the 1980s, for example, spiked by an article in the peer-reviewed *American Journal of Epidemiology*, there was a growing fear that emissions from high-tension wires caused leukemia in young children. Initially, debates about the issue were limited to a few epidemiologists.[11]

Later, articles began to appear in local newspapers, such as *New Haven Register*, *Salisbury* (North Carolina) *Post*, and the *Montecito* (California) *Life*, all writing on reported clusters of leukemia in their community's schoolchildren. Shortly thereafter, the national press (*New York Times*, *Washington Post*, *The Saturday Review*, and *The New Yorker* magazine, for example) began writing on the issue. *Consumer Reports* urged the public to avoid using electric blankets.[12]

Debates between the electrical power industry and environmentalists began to mushroom. Organizations were formed in local communities to confront the power companies. In Seattle, for example, Citizens Against Overhead Power Lines was able to halt construction of power lines. A cottage industry of tort lawyers, engineers who measure energy fields, and writers grew and expanded.

Research reports began to counter the growing perception that overhead power lines were causing leukemia. One study appeared to close out the issue. Conducted by the National Cancer Institute and published in the *New England Journal of Medicine*, the study concluded that there is no evidence that overhead power lines caused cancer.[13]

A subsequent report revealed that the original study that kicked off the issue of power lines causing leukemia was based on falsified data. Nonetheless, there were still critics who were undeterred by the data. One epidemiologist at the University of North Carolina, for example, said the National Cancer Institute study result was not compelling evidence. In another example, the editor of the *Microwave News* claimed it was still an open debate.

The foregoing is a classic example of how a social issue emerges and proceeds through a "life cycle."

1. A structural shift occurs (studies revealing that technology changes can cause environmental problems influence the attitude of the public to the environment);
2. As a consequence, a problem is recognized (reports in technical journals and alternative media suggest a relationship in clusters of childhood cancer, for example, are found near overhead power lines);
3. Organizations become established to debate the issue (Citizens Against Overhead Power Lines);
4. A policy agenda is set and reports are published in the national press. Local and federal governments begin discussing ways to resolve the issue (e.g., require power lines to be built at specified distances from schools);
5. A solution is formalized (law or regulation is promulgated);
6. Penalties are assessed.

The overhead power line issue did not proceed through stages 5 and 6. Nonetheless, it did incur costs. The office of Science and Technology estimated that by 1995, the controversy was costing the American public between $1 and $3 billion in litigation, lost property values, higher utility bills, and relocated power lines.

Monitoring the emergence of social issues is becoming ever more critical as the public becomes increasingly activist. This is clearly evident in the most recent social issue to come under scrutiny—fast-food and soft drink beverage companies. These industries are accused of promoting unhealthy diets resulting in obesity and a rise in diabetes, especially among youngsters.

The industries are accused of using advertising tricks to lure youngsters into eating food with little nutritional value. Some critics complain that the industry falsifies its advertising claims. A few highly publicized lawsuits have been initiated by obese and diabetic consumers. Obesity, in other words, has become a public issue, requiring a public-focused strategy response led by the CEO and the top leadership of fast-food companies.

Taking cues from the tobacco companies' experiences, the fast-food industry launched campaigns to encourage consumers to eat sensibly. It also produced products that were low in calories and cholesterol. Whether or not these efforts succeed is too early to tell. One lesson, however, is that the fast-food industry refuses to enter into a denial phase and has developed programs to respond to the issue and the critics.

That is one of the lessons of managing social issues. Be open, honest, and quick in responding to the concerns of critics. Get the facts and present the case.

A second lesson is to develop ways to identify issues early in their development. Most social issues emerge at the community level. This is where the concerns first become expressed. Issue identification and analysis should be part of a company's community strategy.

Questions that should guide early identification at the community level are: How is the issue being expressed? Are there any organizations involved in the development of the issue? The objective is to stay ahead of the issue pattern of development and respond with appropriate measures. One technique is to use the social issues or corporate citizenship condition letter example described in chapter 9.

The difficulty many managers have to overcome is the personalization of issues. Issues are not right or wrong. It matters little, too, whether the issue is factual or relevant. It is how it is perceived. The way the company responds affects its level of trust with stakeholders. To maintain trust, managers have to deal openly with the perceptions that stakeholders have of the issue.

TRIPLE BOTTOM LINE STRATEGIES

In 1995, Shell Oil Company in the United Kingdom, the largest operating company within the Royal Dutch/Shell Group of companies outside of North America, was forced by Greenpeace to halt its plan to dispose of a used oil rig in the North Atlantic. The repercussions were enormous. Just to change the decision cost the company an additional $200 million. Boycotts and threats against service stations caused huge losses in sales. In one week alone, sales in Germany plummeted below 50 percent.

Later in the same year, the company was also criticized for its failure to stop the Nigerian government from executing a world-renowned writer and environmentalist, Ken Saro-Wiwa, who had been critical of Shell and other oil companies for their devastation of Nigeria.

These two events severely damaged the company's public reputation, admitted its managing director. Employee morale plummeted. Many workers were embarrassed to admit they were Shell employees. But the events had a transformative effect. The company went through considerable soul-searching. It engaged the services of a consulting firm and conducted an exhaustive survey of employees and external stakeholders. While the evidence revealed that the disposal decision was environmentally correct, it was not politically correct. The company, it learned, had neglected taking into account the views of the public and politicians.

Shell moved to adopt a vision of the company that would encompass what is called the triple bottom line—economic, environmental, and social accountability. The concept suggests that a company's new license to operate in the environment of corporate citizenship comes not just from satisfying shareholders and employees through improved profits, it comes also from improving the environment and becoming socially responsible.

It published an annual responsibility report and pledged to use the principles of sustainable development in all its operations—taking account of their social and environmental consequences as well as the economic dimension. The company said it believed its long-term competitive success depends on being trusted to meet society's expectations.

The former chairman of the company's Committee on Managing Directors, Cor Herkstroter who initiated the study, announced, "our [business] decisions need to weigh the sometimes conflicting demands of economic and environment sustainability, and responsibility to the people involved." Recognizing the activist environment within which companies operate, Herkstroter also added that the key challenge will be to do this "in a CNN world."[14]

The company's annual responsibility report detailing its successes and failures in human rights and the impact on the environment has received praise for its openness and honesty. Transparency International, a European watchdog group, claimed no other oil company produces anything as comprehensive and candid about global social responsibility.[15]

The triple bottom line, or sustainability strategy, is a response to activist groups pressuring companies to improve their ethical performance. It is also an avenue for measuring a company's citizenship performance.

PriceWaterhouseCoopers in Australia, for example, conducted a study of the triple bottom line performance of forty of Australia's largest companies. It used the information to analyze how each company used its Concise Annual Report to communicate its triple bottom line reports. They discovered, unfortunately, that companies were more likely to report their social performance than the economic or environmental performance.[16]

While triple bottom line reporting is just emerging, it is in recognition that it is in response to global activists. Protests at the World Trade Organization meetings have forced many companies to explore developing environment sustainability strategies.

SUMMARY

Societal strategies are in different stages of evolution from community strategies. They are emergent and often experimental as companies try to fit their performance to changing sets of concerns and issues, much like the evolution of community strategies in the 1990s.

All too often, companies have relied on community strategies to respond to public or societal concerns. Shell in the United States and the United Kingdom has an excellent community reputation. It has spent time, money, and effort in improving the quality of life in the communities in which it operates. But those efforts and that success could not be used to respond to public issues exploited by Greenpeace.

Successful societal strategies. There are some common elements that make a societal strategy successful.

First, societal strategies can be a response to a challenge to a company's reputation or a marketing opportunity to be seized. Cause-related marketing is an opportunistic strategy. It is a way to sell more products or, indeed, as in the case of Avon, to save a company from failure. Social issues strategies tend to be responsive to threats to a company.

The important point, however, both site community strategies and societal strategies are designed to make a company proactive in its relationships with external stakeholders. The purpose is to avoid crises. A crisis similar to that which beset Shell U.K. is an indication that the company's societal and site community strategies failed.

Second, a societal strategy has to be spearheaded and supported by the CEO. This is not a new mandate. As I pointed out in the Preface, as far back as the 1970s, Peter Drucker pointed out that managing a company's social impacts and social responsibilities was one of the three essential tasks of managers.

In an activist society, the responsibility for leading and managing corporate citizenship falls to the CEO. The CEO sets the business and social vision and the strategies for the way the visions are carried out. The CEO is being held accountable by societies for the responsible behavior of the company's social impacts and social responsibilities.

It is significant that successful site and societal community strategies invariably have the heavy involvement of the CEO. A strategy initiated by the CEO, such as that started by Gerstner of IBM, had a distinct advantage. It was bound to get the attention of company managers. That alone did not make IBM On Demand Community successful. But it was a great start.

Third, the CEO has to sustain the strategy efforts and drive it down into the culture of the organization. If not, once the CEO leaves the company, there is a tendency for the strategy to disappear. Consider, for example, Stride Rite. In the 1990s, Arnold Hiatt, the CEO of Stride Rite, a manufacturer of children's shoes for eighty-five years, was lionized in the press for his corporate community relations initiatives, and rightly so. Despite criticism from some business associates and even members of his board, Hiatt persisted in developing imaginative and sometimes even controversial community involvement programs.

At the company's plant in Boston's inner city, for example, Hiatt opened up a day care program for the employees. He also extended the day care facilities to the children in the neighborhood, to the consternation of many employees. Most of the neighborhood children were poor and on public assistance. Hiatt refused to alter the program. He did succeed in changing the views of the employees and made the day care program a success.

When he began a day care facility for employees at the company headquarters in Cambridge, he made it unique by inviting elderly residents to share the day care facilities with the children, another innovation for which he was widely praised. He encouraged college students to be engaged in volunteer programs in the inner city. In turn, the company provided scholarships to the students.

Once Hiatt retired, however, the programs disappeared. Unlike Gerstner, no efforts were made to institutionalize the program within the company. No one was around to carry on the Hiatt legacy.

Fourth, while the CEO has implicit responsibility for the management of the company's charitable programs, he or she needs to maintain a distance from charitable decisions to protect the integrity of those decisions. The days when the CEO was the dispenser of a company's largess is over. Today, the CEO is likely to generate criticism and damage the reputation of the company in charitable decisions.

The actions of Sanford Weill, chairman of Citigroup, is a case example. In 1999, Weill was negotiating with AT&T to sell a block of its shares. Citigroup's telecommunications stock analyst, Jack Grubman, had been giving the company negative ratings. Weill asked Grubman to "relook" at his consistently negative ratings of AT&T stock. Grubman, at the time, was unsuccessfully trying to get his two children admitted into the highly selective (supposedly harder to get into than Harvard) 92nd Street Y nursery school. Weill, as Grubman knew, was friendly with some of the 92nd Street Y's board members.

Grubman changed his rating of AT&T's stock from neutral to buy. Citigroup in the summer of 2000 donated $1 million to the 92nd Street Y. Shortly thereafter, Grubman's children received an acceptance into the nursery school. In an e-mail to a colleague, Grubman boasted, "I used Sandy to get my kids in the 92nd St. Y preschool . . . once the coast was clear . . . I went back to my normal negative self on T."[17]

During this period, AT&T stock lost 50 percent of its value. Some $80 billion in market value just vanished.[18]

There are other equally shameful examples. Tyco International admits that it donated more than $600 million of corporate funds to a variety of charities to promote the image of its former chairman, Dennis Kozlowski. James Agee, the wonder boy of corporate management in the 1980s, appointed his wife, Mary Cunningham, to chair the Morris Knudsen Company's charitable foundation. Grants were given to charities personally favored by Agee and Cunningham—anti-abortion and Catholic organizations. Computer Associates donated more than $40 million to the State University of New York, whose president was on the board.

Surprisingly, this behavior is tolerated. The president of Fleckenstein Capital reported, "[T]his was standard practice on Wall Street in the '90s. The only reason we got to know about this was a paper trail."[19]

In an activist society, such actions by CEOs have negative consequences. They can damage the reputation of both the company and CEO. A publisher, for example, has decided not to release an autobiography written by Weill because of the adverse publicity surrounding his involvement in the Grubman affair. Weill also lost his chance of being appointed to the board of the New York Stock Exchange allegedly because of the incident.

The lesson is clear. The CEO should stick to leading and managing the corporate citizenship strategies.

Fifth, one distinguishing feature of most societal strategies is that they are industry specific. Indeed, some are company specific. Anheuser-Busch's responsible-drinking strategy, of course, is useful for the alcohol beverage industry. Philip Morris, however, has a strategy to persuade people to give up smoking—oddly, the only company that discourages consumers from using its product. No other tobacco company employs that strategy.

Sixth, link the societal strategy with the site community strategy. The societal strategy is a community strategy. Admittedly, it is a community far different and more complex than a site community. Building face-to-face working relationships with site community stakeholders is the primary program of a site community strategy.

Companies often have to rely on communication strategies to build relationships or promote the citizenship reputation of the company. Nonetheless, linking the site and societal strategy with a program strengthens both strategies. When IBM, for example, launched its IBM On Demand Community program, it promoted volunteer events in over ninety countries. By November 2003, the company had over 12,000 employees registered in its volunteer programs.

Seventh, do not give senior executives a free pass on training. Frequently, senior executives do not pay heed to carrying out the public strategy the company has adopted.

Shell U.K. provides an excellent example. It spent a considerable sum of money and the time of many managers to transform the company from being indifferent to public concerns to one that insisted it would be in the forefront of addressing the emerging concerns of an activist world.

It promoted this vision to managers and employees in its locations throughout the world. It publicized its program with brochures and newspaper releases. A few senior executives apparently did not understand the implications of the reformulated strategy of the triple bottom line that emphasized ethics and openness in running the company. In an attempt to present a more positive outlook to stockholders, the company's officers published false statements on petroleum reserves in 2003. The incident led to the resignation of the company's top officers, including its chairman, Sir Philip Watts, who led the transformation study and the development of the triple bottom line strategy.

General Electric has made training of managers a prime strategy in its new corporate citizenship efforts. Jeffrey Immelt, CEO of General Electric, has appointed the company's chief learning officer, Robert Corcoran, to vice president of corporate citizenship. Corcoran makes presentations to managers at the company's highly regarded Crotonville Management Development Center. Putting corporate citizenship on the agenda at Crotonville sends a message about the importance to Immelt and to General Electric.

Eight, when developing a societal community strategy, learn from the example of the efforts that went into designing site community strategies. Move incrementally and share experiences and practices among the company's managers.

Experience in the development of business strategies suggests that in a changing, uncertain, and turbulent environment, the development of a company's strategies should be cautious and piece by piece. The research of James Bryant Quinn, Dartmouth's Tuck Business School professor, indicates that successful strategies tend to evolve incrementally.[20] They should be viewed as part of a work in progress, evolving carefully and certainly.

Notes

PREFACE

1. W. Safire, "Essay on the New Socialism," *New York Times*, February 26, 1996.

2. D. Cogman and J. M. Oppenheim, "Controversy Incorporated," *The McKinsey Quarterly*, no. 4 (2002): p. 57.

3. M. E. Porter and M. R. Kramer, "The Competitive Advantage of Corporate Philanthropy," *Harvard Business Review* 80, no. 12 (December 2002): pp. 56–69.

CHAPTER 1

1. S. H. Verhovek, "Radical Animal Rights Groups Step up Protests," *New York Times*, November 11, 2001, p. A16.

2. "Too Much Corporate Power?" *BusinessWeek*, September 11, 2000, pp. 144–58.

3. J. E. Stiglitz, *Globalization and Its Discontents* (New York: The New Press, 1998), p. xxxiii.

4. Ibid., p. 145.

5. J. Kahn, "Trade Talks Hinge on Fitness of U.S.," *New York Times*, November 10, 2001, p. A6.

6. G. Hall, "Interview of Lester Salamon," *The Johns Hopkins Gazette Online*, January 3, 2000.

7. The Center for Corporate Citizenship at Boston College, *Community Relations Index, 2001* (Chestnut Hill, MA: The Center for Corporate Citizenship at Boston College, 2001).

8. "Corporate Giving Low on Mayors' Priority List," *Community Relations Letter* 4, no. 2 (October 1989).

9. M. Hirsh, "Protesting Plutocracy," *Newsweek*, December 2000–February 2001, p. 67.

10. "Leaner Times in Albany," *New York Times*, April 13, 2000, p. A26.

11. J. Vennochi, "It's Appearance, Stupid," *Boston Globe*, December 4, 1998.

12. J. Welch (with Jack J. Byrne) *Jack, Straight from the Gut* (New York: Warner Business Books, 2001), p. 294.

13. This is a variation of Peter Drucker's five questions for organizations, namely, What is our mission? Who are our customers? What are our results? What is our plan?

14. R. Fisher and E. Shrage, "Challenging Community Organizing: Facing the 21st Century," *Journal of Community Practice* 8, no. 3 (2000): pp. 1–19.

15. M. Castells, *The Information Age Economy, Society and Culture, Vol. I: The Rise of the Network Society* (Cambridge, MA: Blackwell, 1996).

CHAPTER 2

1. J. E. Stiglitz, *Globalization and Its Discontents* (New York: The New Press, 1998), pp. xxi–xxii.

2. See doctoral disseration, "The Study of Planning and Implementing Processes in Social Welfare by Two Voluntary Organizations," 1962 by Mary Ella Robertson, University of Pittsburgh, describing how Pittsburgh power structure members resolved conflicts with each other.

3. E. M. Burke, *A Participatory Approach to Urban Planning* (New York: Human Sciences Press, 1979), pp. 30–31.

4. Foundation for Public Affairs, *Public Interest Profiles, 1998–1999* (Washington, D.C.: Congressional Quarterly Inc., 1998).

5. See, for example, F. Fisher and E. Shragge, "Challenging Community Organizing: Facing the 21st Century," *Journal of Community Practice* 8, no. 3 (2000): pp. 1–19.

6. P. J. Simmons, "Learning to Live with NGOs" *Foreign Policy* (fall 1998): p. 83.

7. J. M. Berry, *The New Liberalism: The Rising Power of Citizen Groups* (Washington, D.C.: The Brookings Institution Press, 1999), p. 48.

8. Ibid., p. 2.

9. A. H. Maslow, *Motivation and Personality* (New York: Harper & Brothers, 1954).

10. Grey Advertising, Inc., *Grey Matter Alert No. 3: Today's Americans in Tough Times and Beyond* (New York: Grey Advertising, 1991), p. 4.

11. R. L. Gildea, "Consumer Survey Confirms Corporate Social Action Affects Buying Decisions," *Public Relations Quarterly* 39 (winter 1994–1995) and Council on Foundations, *Measuring Value of Corporate Citizenship* (Washington, D.C.: Council on Foundations, 1996).

12. R. Milloy, "Texans Split Over Plan to Reopen Pipeline," *New York Times*, January 18, 2000, p. A12.

13. M.v.N. Whitman, *New World, New Rules: The Changing Role of the American Corporation* (Boston: Harvard Business School Press), pp. 10–11.

14. T. L. Friedman, The Lexus and the Olive Tree (New York: Farrar Straus Giroux, 1999) p. 162.

15. The Conference Board, *Across the Board*, July/August, 2000.

16. T. L. Friedman, "Surfing the Wetlands," *New York Times*, August 8, 1998, p. 27A.

17. B. Lynn, "Going Green in Shades of Gray," *America Way*, March 15, 2001, p. 105.

18. White House, Executive Order 12329, "President's Task Force on Private Sector Initiatives," Washington, D.C., 1991.

19. "J. Garten: The Thought Leader Interview," *Strategy and Business* 22 (first quarter, 2001): pp. 171–77.

20. Council on Foundations, *The Climate for Giving: Current and Future CEOs Talk About "Giving" in Today's Environment* (Washington, D.C.: Council on Foundations, 1988), pp. 14–15.

21. C. Reidy and T. C. Palmer Jr., "Give Me More," *Boston Globe*, June 15, 2003, p. J 1.

22. *Business Ethics* (fall 2002): p. 9.

23. From W. Hodges, *Company and Community* (New York: Harper & Brothers, 1958), p. 3.

CHAPTER 3

1. N. Onishi, "As Oil Riches Flow, Poor Village Cries Out," *New York Times*, December 22, 2002, p. 15.

2. Greenpeace Web page, http://www.greenpeace.org.

3. Letter to author, June 16, 1997.

4. Business in the Community, "Seeing Is Believing Programme Report," 1994, p. 2.

5. D. H. Smith, "The Philanthropy Business," *Society* 15, no. 2 (January/February 1978).

6. Quoted in M. Specter, "The Extremist: The Woman Behind the Most Successful Radical Group in America," *The New Yorker*, April 14, 2003, p. 66.

7. M. Specter, "The Extremist: The Woman Behind the Most Successful Radical Group in America," *The New Yorker*, April 14, 2003, p. 67.

8. "Lung Association Faults U.S. on Enforcing Clean Air Laws," *New York Times*, May 5, 2002, p. A20.

9. F. Bruni, "At 10, Act Up Doesn't Much, Anymore," *New York Times*, March 21, 1997.

10. For more about social connectors, see M. Gladwell, *The Tipping Point: How Little Things Can Made a Big Difference* (Boston: Little, Brown and Company, 2000).

CHAPTER 4

1. E. M. Burke, "A Social Vision," *New York Times*, February 18, 1990. See also, E. M. Burke, *Corporate Community Relations: The Principle of the Neighbor of Choice* (Westport, CT: Praeger, 1999).

2. Boston College, Center for Corporate Community Relations, *Making the Business Case: Determining the Value of Corporate Community Involvement* (Chestnut Hill, MA: Boston College, Center for Corporate Community Relations, 2000).

3. J. A. Ledingham and S. D. Bruning, "Relationship Management in Public Relations: Dimensions of an Organizational Public Relationship," *Public Relations Review* 34, no.1 (spring 1998): pp. 55–65.

4. F. Norris and S. Day, "Coke to Report Stock Options as Expenses," *New York Times*, July 15, 2002, pp. A1, A13.

5. M. Lipton, "Demystifying the Development of an Organizational Vision," *Sloan Management Review* (summer 1996): p. 84.

6. J. Nocera, "The Customer Is Usually Right: Jack Welch Looks Back over His 20 Years at the Helm of G.E.," *The New York Times Book Review*, October 14, 2001, p. 13.

7. W. Bennis, "Will the Legacy Live On," *Harvard Business Review* (February 2002): p. 99.

8. The Business Roundtable, "Statement on Corporate Responsibility" (Washington, D.C.: The Business Roundtable, 1981), also cited in I. Wilson, *The New Rules of Corporate Conduct: Rewriting the Social Charter* (Westport, CT: Quorum Books, 2000), p. 12.

9. J. Welch (with J. A. Byrne), *Jack: Straight from the Gut* (New York: Warner Business Books, 2001), p. 108.

10. Ibid., p. 109.

11. *New York Times*, May 12, 2000, and May 15, 2000.

12. M. Lipton, "Demystifying the Development of an Organizational Vision," p. 85.

13. K. Eichenwald, "Biotechnology Food: From the Lab to a Debacle," *New York Times*, January 25, 2001, p. 1, C6–C7.

14. R. B. Shapiro, *The Welcome Tension of Technology: The Need for Dialogue about Agricultural Biotechnology* (St. Louis: Center for the Study of American Business, CEO Series 37, February 2000), p. 4.

CHAPTER 5

1. This case example is taken from a book written by the company's CEO, Michael Eisner. Unless otherwise noted, all quotes are from a chap-

ter in Eisner's book. M. D. Eisner, *Work in Progress* (New York: Random House, 1999), pp. 319–38.

2. M. D. Eisner, "Disney's Virginia Park Will Bring American Experience to Life," *New York Times*, July 23, 1993.

3. R. Turner, "Disney Hopes Retreat Is Better Part of Public Relation," *Wall Street Journal*, September 30, 1994.

4. *New York Times*, "Disney Retreats at Bull Run," September 30, 1994 p. 30A.

5. T. F. O'Boyle, *At Any Cost: Jack Welch, General Electric, and the Pursuit of Profit* (New York: Alfred A. Knopf, 1998), p. 188.

6. Ibid., pp. 193–202.

7. J. Welch (with J. A. Byrne), *Jack: Straight from the Gut* (New York: Warner Business Books, 2001), pp. 288–90.

8. J. Welch, *Jack*, p. 293.

9. M. Cohen, "G.E. Accused of Delay Tactic," *Boston Globe*, October 19, 1997, p. B1, B6.

10. T. F. O'Boyle, *At Any Cost*, p. 198.

11. Ibid., p. 190.

12. P. J. Howe, "A Personal Link in Pittsfield," *Boston Globe*, May 14, 1998, p. B1.

13. T. F. O'Boyle, *At Any Cost.*, p. 189.

14. E. Goldschnieder, "At G.E., Former Enemies Are Now Employees," *Boston Globe*, August 6, 2000, p. B4.

15. "Mrs. Whitman Stays the Course," *New York Times*, August 2, 2001, p. A20.

16. J. Welch, *Jack*, p. 283.

17. L. Susskind uses the acronym D-A-D, which according to Susskind was first used by Dan Dudek in a doctoral dissertation.

18. T. F. O'Boyle, *At Any Cost*, p. 206.

19. J. Welch, *Jack*, p. 283–94.

20. E. Kolbert, "The Nun vs. the C.E.O. in a Fight Over PCBs," *New York Times*, May 25, 1998, p. A16.

21. P. M. Sandman, Speech at Center for Corporate Citizenship Conference, March 31, 2004, San Francisco, CA.

22. D. McGregor, *The Human Side of Enterprise* (New York: McGraw-Hill Book Company, Inc., 1960), pp. 33–44. Also, A. H. Maslow, *Motivation and Personality*, 2nd ed. (New York: Harper & Row Publishers, 1970), pp. 35–58.

23. A. Wolfe, *One Nation After All: What Middle Class Americans Really Think About: God, Country, Family, Racism, Welfare, Immigration, Homosexuality, Work, The Right, The Left, and Each Other* (New York: Viking, 2000), p. 320.

24. Ibid., pp. 249–50.

25. P. J. Howe, "A Personal Link in Pittsfield," *Boston Globe*, May 14, 1998, p. B1.

26. "Camden Environmental Suit to be Heard," *New York Times*, September 25, 2001, p. A26.

27. K. Auletta, "Final Offer: What Kept Microsoft from Settling Its Case?" *The New Yorker*, January 15, 2001, p. 41.

CHAPTER 6

1. Merck uses this term that is believed to be first coined by Dan Dudek in a doctoral dissertation. See L. Susskind.

2. I. Peterson, "A Company Move That Hasn't Irked the Neighbors," *New York Times*, November 15, 1992, pp. 52, 54.

3. Merck & Co., Inc., *A Guide to Becoming a Neighbor of Choice* (Whitehouse Station, NJ: Merck and Co., 1997) p. 9.

4. C. Campbell, "Dam Battle Heats Up," *The Maple Ridge-Pitt Meadows Times*, July 16, 1995.

5. Ibid.

6. See, for example, my own research on this subject: E. Burke, "Citizen Participation Strategies," *Journal of the American Institute of Planners* xxxiv, no. 5 (September 1968): pp. 287–94.

7. Province of British Columbia, *Water Use Plan Guidelines* (Canadian Cataloguing in Publication Data: British Columbia, December 1998).

8. K. Mark, "Deal Heals River Wounds," *The Maple Ridge-Pitt Meadows Times*, December 28, 1997.

9. B.C. Hydro, *Stave River Water Use Plan: Report of the Consultative Committee*, prepared by L. Falling, M.R.M., P. Eng., Compass Resource Management Ltd.

10. D. Goleman, *Working with Emotional Intelligence* (New York: Bantam Books, 1998), pp. 24–28.

CHAPTER 7

1. R. E. Freeman, *Strategic Management: A Stakeholder Approach* (New York: Basic Books, 1984).

2. Columbia University, Bureau of Applied Social Research, *The Volunteers: Means and Ends in a National Organization*, a report by David L. Sill (Glencoe, IL: Free Press, 1957).

3. Market and Communications Research, Inc., *Monsanto Company, Muscatine Area Survey June 2000* (Rockville, MD: Market and Communications Research, Inc., July 2000), p. 1.

4. P. M. Sandman, Speech at Center for Corporate Citizenship at Boston College Conference, March 31, 2004, San Francisco, CA.

CHAPTER 8

1. Market and Communications Research, Inc., *Monsanto Company, Muscatine Area Survey June 2000* (Rockville, MD: Market and Communications Research, Inc., July 2000), p. 1.

2. Ibid., pp. 20–21.

3. Merck & Co., Inc., *A Guide to Becoming a Neighbor of Choice* (Whitehouse Station, NJ: Merck & Co. Inc., 1997), pp. 10–12.

4. Ibid., p. 11.

5. D. Goleman, *Working with Emotional Intelligence* (New York: Bantam Books, 1998), pp. 26–27 and 169–95. See also, D. Goleman, "What Makes a Leader," *Harvard Business Review* (November–December 1998): pp. 92–102.

6. S. D. Bruning and J. A. Ledingham, "Ten Guidelines for Effectively Managing the Organization-Public Relationship," in *Business Research Yearbook*, eds. J. Bilerman and A. Alkhafaji (Salina, MI: McNaughton & Gunn, Inc., 1998), pp. 776–80.

CHAPTER 9

1. J. C. Worthy, "Organizational Structure and Employee Morale," *American Sociological Review* 15, no. 2 (April 1950): pp. 169–79.

2. R. Trabert, "How to Develop an External Relations Plan," The Center for Corporate Citizenship at Boston College, Web page, http://www.bc.edu/centers/ccc.

CHAPTER 11

1. D. P. Baron, "Going Head to Head," *Stanford Social Innovation Review*, p. 38.

2. Ibid., p. 39.

3. R. E. Evans, "Community Relations: The Key to Operations Success" (speech presented at the 1993 Community Relations Leaders Conference sponsored by The Center for Corporate Community Relations at Boston College, Chicago, 1993).

4. E. M. Burke, *Corporate Community Relations: The Principle of the Neighbor of Choice* (Westport, CT: Praeger, 1999).

5. Canadian Imperial Bank of Commerce, CIBC Community Relations Handbook (Calgary, Canada: CIBC, 1997).

6. C. J. Fombrun, *Reputation: Realizing the Value from Corporate Image* (Boston, MA: Harvard Business School Press, 1996), pp. 187–90.

7. See H. Levinson, *Psychological Man* (Cambridge, MA: The Levinson Institute, 1976), pp. 90–91.

8. See E. M. Burke, *Corporate Community Relations: The Principle of the Neighbor of Choice*, for a fuller description of the principle of the psychological contract.

9. Ibid., p. 91.

10. A. Naude, "Let's Get Local: Chemical Companies Community Outreach Programs," *Chemical Marketing Reporter*, October 13, 1994.

11. Center for Corporate Community Relations at Boston College, "Paper Examines Good Relationship between Community Group and Bristol-Myers Squibb—and How It Got That Way," *Community Relations Letter* 12, no. 2 (October, 1997): p. 3.

12. Market and Communications Research, Inc., *Monsanto Company Muscatine Area Survey, June 2000* (Rockville, MD: Market and Communications Research, Inc., 2000), p. 14.

13. Merck, *A Guide to Becoming a Neighbor of Choice* (Whitehouse Station, NJ: Merck & Co., 1997), p. 25.

14. L. V. Gerstner, Jr., *Who Says Elephants Can't Dance* (New York: Harper Business, 2002), p. 276.

15. Motorola 2002 Corporate Citizenship Report (Schaumburg, IL: Motorola, Inc.), p. 17.

16. E. M. Burke, *Corporate Community Relations*, pp. 144–47.

17. J. A. Ledingham and S. D. Bruning, "Building Loyalty through Community Relations," *Public Relations Strategist* 2, no. 2 (September 1997): pp. 27–29.

18. Merck, *A Guide to Becoming a Neighbor of Choice*, p. 12.

19. M. E. Porter and C.V.D. Linde, "Green and Competitive," *Harvard Business Review on Business and the Environment* (Boston: Harvard Business School Press, 2000), p. 148.

CHAPTER 12

1. D. B. Turbam and D. W. Greening, "Corporate Social Performance and Organizational Attractiveness to Prospective Employees," *Academy of Management Journal* 40, no. 9 (June 1997): p. 663.

2. J. F. Kaabs, "Community Service Helps UPS Develop Managers," *Personnel Journal*, October 1993, pp. 90–98.

3. S. Caudron, "Volunteer Efforts Offer Low-Cost Training Options," *Personal Journal*, June 1944, pp. 38–43.

4. P. F. Drucker, *Managing in a Time of Great Change* (New York: Truman Talley Books/Dutton, 1995), p. 344.

5. Pillsbury Employee Volunteer Program, "Development through Volunteerism: Growing Professionally . . . Serving the Community" (Minneapolis, MN: The Pillsbury Company, n.d.).

6. W. Hodges, *Company and Community: Case Studies in Industry-City Relationships,* (New York: Harper and Brothers, 1958), p. 299, and Market

and Communications Research, Inc., Monsanto Company: Muscatine (Iowa) Survey, June 2000 (Rockville, MD: Market and Communications Research, Inc., 2000) are two examples.

7. L. V. Gerstner, Jr., *Who Says Elephants Can't Dance?: Inside IBM's Historic Turnaround* (New York: Harper Business Books, 2002), p. 277.

8. B. Davenport, "Corporate Citizenship: A Stakeholder Approach for Defining Corporate Social Performance and Identifying Measures for Assessing It," *Business and Society*, June 2000, pp. 210–19.

9. C. J. Fombrun, *Reputation: Realizing the Value from the Corporate Image* (Boston: Harvard Business School Press, 1996).

10. J. F. Boren, *Community Relations 1987: A Profile of the Profession* (Chestnut Hill, MA: The Center for Corporate Community Relations at Boston College, 1987).

11. M. E. Porter and C.V.D. Linde, "Green and Competitive," *Harvard Business Review on Business and the Environment* (Boston: Harvard Business School Press, 2000), p. 153.

CHAPTER 13

1. P. Brogran, "Some Colleges Say No to Mixing Beer, Sports," *Honolulu Advertiser*, March 28, 2004.

2. "Teens and Booze," *The Washington Post*, September 22, 2003, p. A22.

3. L. V. Gerstner, Jr., *Who Says Elephants Can't Dance?* (New York: Harper Business Books, 2002), p. 273.

4. S. Adkins, *Cause Related Marketing: Who Cares Wins* (Oxford, England: Butterworth-Heinemann, 1999), pp. 65–70.

5. P. R. Varadaraja and A. Menon, "Cause-Related Marketing: A Co-alignment of Marketing Strategy and Corporate Philanthropy," *Journal of Marketing* 52 (July 1988): p. 60.

6. S. M. Smith and D. S. Alcorn, "Cause Marketing: A New Direction in the Marketing of Corporate Responsibility," *Journal of Services Marketing* 8, no. 3 (1991): p. 26.

7. S. Adkins, *Cause Related Marketing: Who Cares Wins.*

8. Ibid., p. 138.

9. Ibid., pp. 194–96.

10. Ibid., p. 204.

11. N. Wertheimer and E. Leeper, "Electric Writing Configurations and Childhood Cancer," *American Journal of Epidemiology* (March 1997): pp. 273–84.

12. S. Schiefelbein, "The Invisible Threat: The Stifled Story of Electric Waves," *The Saturday Review*, 1979, pp. 16–29; P. Brodeur, "Annals of Radiation: The Hazards of Electromagnetic Fields," *New Yorker*, June 12, 1989, pp. 51–88; and P. Brodeur, "Annals of Radiation, Cancer and Power

Lines: Calamity on Meadows Street," *New Yorker*, July 1990, pp. 38–72; R. L. Park, "Power Line Paranoia," *New York Times*, November 13, 1996, p. A23.

13. M. S. Linet, et al., "Residential Exposure to Magnetic Fields and Acute Lymphoblastic Leukemia in Children," *New England Journal of Medicine* 337, July 3, 1997, pp. 1–7.

14. *The CEO Agenda* (London, England: SustainAbility Ltd., 1998), p. 12.

15. "Interview with Cor Herkstroter," *Financial Times* (London), May 10, 1996, and letter from H. C. Rothermund, Managing Director, Shell U.K. to author, June 16, 1997.

16. M. Newson, "Australia's Triple Bottom Line Performance, PriceWaterhouseCoopers," Australia report, 2004.

17. "Analyst Boasted of Preschool Deal," *Boston Globe*, April 29, 2003, p. D7.

18. S. Strom, "Private Preschool Admissions: Grease and the City," *New York Times*, November 16, 2002, p. B1.

19. G. Morgenson, "Does the Rot on Wall Street Reach Right to the Top?" *New York Times*, November 17, 2002, p. 1bu.

20. J.B. Quinn, *Strategies for Change: Logical Incrementalism* (Homewood, IL: Irwin, 1980).

Name Index

Abbot Corporation, 136

Act Up, 43, 44

Adams, Charles Francis, 23

Adkins, Susan, 161

Agent Orange, 5, 82, 169

Allen, George, 58, 59

Allyn, Stanley, 27

Alouette River Stakeholder Committee, 74

American Cancer Society, 15, 43

American Express, 160

American Journal of Epidemiology, 163

American Lung Association, 15, 43

American Meat Institute Foundation, 40

American Medical Association, 82

Amoco, 124

Anderson, Ray, 23

Anheuser-Busch, 123, 156, 157, 170

Animal Liberation Front, 3

Annan, Kofi, 54

Arthur Andersen, 6

Association of British Insurers, 2

AT&T, 29, 30, 131, 143, 169

Atsepoyi, Alicia (Mama Ayo), 32, 33, 36, 44

Avon, 161, 162, 167

Babbit, Bruce, 59

Bank of America, 131–32

Barclays Bank, 47

Baxter International, 2

BC Hydro, 51, 73–77, 130

Beckman, Alan, 103–5

Ben & Jerry's Ice Cream, 24

Bennis, Warren, 49, 67

Berry, Jeffrey, 17–18

Boeing Company, 20

Bonsignore, Michael, 19–20

Bossidy, Lawrence, 20

Boston College Graduate School of Social Work, xi

Boston Globe, 6

Bothwell, Robert, 38

Boy Scouts of America, 132

BP Oil Comapny, 8, 20, 24

Brent Spar, 33–34, 43

Bristol-Myers Squibb, 84, 138, 148

Browne, John, 24

Bruning, Stephen, 96, 97, 128

Buchanan, Patrick, 21

Burger King, 20, 40, 42

Burke, Edmund, M., 174 n.3, 176 n.1, 178 n.6, 179 n.4, 180 n.8

Burns, Ken, 58
Bush, George W., 5, 15, 19, 22, 60, 61
Business for Social Responsibility (BSR), 25
Business in the Community (BITC), 11, 25, 35–36, 161
Business Roundtable, 6, 49
BusinessWeek, 3

Canadian Imperial Bank of Commerce, 125
Capitol University (Ohio), 95
Carnegie Foundation for International Peace, 16
Carter, Jimmy, xi
Carville, James, 1, 7
Celluci, A. Paul, 61, 65
The Center for Corporate Citizenship at Boston College, xi, 25, 40, 46, 55, 104, 105, 110, 113, 142, 148
Center for Disease Control and Prevention, U.S., 162
Center on Alcohol Marketing and Youth at Georgetown University, 156
Charlie Rose Show, 7
Chemical Manufactures Association, 129
Chevron/Texaco, 3, 31–33
Citigroup, 169
Citizens Against Overhead Power Lines, 163, 164
Clayton, Geoff, 75
Clinton, William, 60–61
CNN, 36, 37
Coca-Cola Company, 47, 123
Coggin, Dana, 31
Committee for Responsive Philanthropy, 37–40, 43
Computer Associates, 169
COMSAT, 88
Cone Public Affairs, 162

Consumer Reports, 163
Corcoran, Robert, 171
Corretti, Patrick, 71–72
Council on Foundations, 24
Cramer, Ann W., 159
Cunningham, Mary, 169

Daft, Douglas, 47
Davis, Robert, 25
De Tocqueville, Alexis, 14
Diageo, 20
Drucker, Peter, 1, 140, 168

Earth Liberation Front, 3
Eisner, Michael, 1, 57–64, 95
Enron, 4, 6, 142
Environmental Protection Agency (U.S.), 61–62
Esber, Suzanne Hoffman, 103
European Commission, 2, 67
Evans, Richard, 124
Express Scripts, 8
Exxon Valdez, 4
ExxonMobil, 2, 58

Falun Gong, 23
Fleckenstein Capital, 169
Fleet Financial Group, 2, 6
Fluor Corporation 8, 102–5
Fombrun, Charles J., 148
Ford Motor Company, 8, 23, 51, 52, 143
Ford, William Clay, 24
Fortune, 49, 125
Fowler, Gail, 71–72
Franklin, John Hope, 58
Freeman, R. Edward, 79
Freeport-MacMoRan Company, 143
Friedman, Thomas, 22, 23

Galbraith, John Kenneth, 59
Gap Company, 2
Garten, Jeffrey, ix
Gates, William, 67

General Electric Company, 3, 7–8, 20, 60, 66, 95, 112, 140, 171
General Motors, 21
Genzyme, 143
Gerstner, Louis V., Jr., 134, 147, 158–60, 168
Goleman, Daniel, 94–95
Goodwin, Robert, 141
Greene, John, 24
Greenpeace, 2, 15, 22, 33, 43, 81, 165, 167
Gregory, Robin, 74
Grey Advertising, 18
Greyhound Bus Company, 2
Grove, Andrew, 36
Grubman, Jack, 169–70

Habitat for Humanity, 16
Hamilton, Scott, 161
Harvard Business School, 16, 21, 94, 126, 137
Herkstroter, Cor, 166
Heublin Company, 123
Hewitt Associates, 139
Hewlitt-Packard (HP), 8, 24
Hiatt, Arnold, 24–25, 168
Honeywell International Corporation, 19–20, 49, 67
Hoover Company, 20

IBM, 8, 37, 134, 145–48, 158–60, 168, 170
Immelt, Jeffrey, 171
Intel, 36–37
Interface Company, 23
Iroquois Pipe Line, 1

Jackson, Judge Thomas Pennfield, 67
Jackson, Rev. Jesse, 123–24, 157
Jazinowski, Jerry, 3
John Hancock Insurance Company, 143
Johnson & Johnson Company, 51, 55

Jones, Reginald, 49–50
J.P. Morgan Chase Company, 142–43

Kerry, John, 22
KFC Company, 40
Kodak, 130
Kozlowski, Dennis, 169
Krueger, Scott, 155–56

Leadership Forum, 25
League of Women Voters, 130
Ledingham, John, 96, 97, 129
Leidy, Mark, 111
Levi Strauss, 132
Levi Strauss Foundation, 25
Levinson, Harry, 126–27
Litow, Stanley, 159
Liz Claiborne, 2
Lloyds Bank of Scotland, 55

Major, John, 34
Mandela, Nelson, 54
Market and Communications Research, Inc., 93
Markey, Edward, 88
Maslow, Abraham, 18
Matalin, Mary, 59
Maytag Company, 20
Mazurki, Joanne, 162
McCullough, David, 58
McDaniels, Timothy, 74
McDonald's, 3, 16, 40, 41, 51
McKinsey and Company, ix
McLaughlin, Peter, 20
MCI, 142
Merck & Company, Inc., 46–47, 69–73, 77, 93–96, 109, 131, 135
Michigan Automotive Compressor Company, 51
Microsoft Company, 6
Microwave News, 164
Middleton, Peter, 47

MIT, 155–56
Mitsubishi Company, 2
Moe, Richard, 58
Monsanto, 2, 52–53, 86, 92, 111, 130–31, 136
Montecito Life (CA), 163
Morris Knudsen Company, 169
Mothers Against Drunk Driving, 83
Motorola Company, 134
Moyers, William, 59

Nader, Ralph, 21
National Alliance for Business, 144
National Alliance of Breast Cancer Organizations, 162
National Association of Manufacturers, 3
National Basketball Association, 41
National Cancer Institute (U.S.), 163–64
National Governor's Association, 158
National Institutes of Health (U.S.), 162
National Rifle Association, 81
National Trust for Historical Preservation, 58
New England Journal of Medicine, 61, 163
New England Patriots, 64–65
New Haven Register, 163
New York Stock Exchange, 2, 170
New York Times, 22, 23, 44, 52, 59, 63, 72, 163
New Yorker, 42, 163
Newkirk, Ingrid, 42
Newsweek, 6
Nike, 2
92nd Street Y, 169
Nocera, Joseph, 49

Office of Science and Technology (U.S.), 164

Ohio Bell Telephone Company, 24
Opinion Research Corporation, 141
O'Reilly, John J., 33

Packard, David, 24
Palmisano, Samuel J., 159
Pannell, Jo, 29, 30, 36
Pataki, George, 61, 63, 65
People for the Ethical Treatment of Animals (PETA), 40, 41, 42, 43, 81
Pepsi Cola Company, 2
Philip Morris Company, 6, 170
Pickle, J.J., 18–19
Pillsbury Company, 140–41, 150
Planned Parenthood, 131
Points of Light Foundation, 141
Polaroid Corporation, 137
Porter, Michael, ix, 137, 149
PriceWaterhouseCoopers, 167
Prince of Wales, 11, 25, 35
Public Affairs Foundation, 15

Quinn, James Bryant, 171

Ramsey, Stephen D., 62
Rand Institute for Social Justice, 137
Raytheon Company, 23
Reagan, Ronald, 11, 12, 144
Reebok Company, 2
Reilly Industries, 130
Rice, Susan, 55
Robertson, Mary Ella, 174 n.2
Robson, Gord, 73
Rothermond, Heinz, 34
Royal Dutch Shell, 51

Safire, William, ix
Salamon, Lester, 5
Salisbury Post (NC), 163
Sandman, Peter, 65, 87
Saro-Wiwa, Ken, 166
Saturday Review, 163

Sears Roebuck and Company, 101–2
Seven-Up, 123
Shapiro, Robert, 52–53
Shawmut Bank, 6
Shell, U.K., 2, 3, 8, 22, 33–34, 43, 165–67, 170
Shell, U.S., 167
Sierra Club, 23, 73
Sirota, Alper & Pfau, 5
Smith, Orin, 8
Society for the Prevention of Cruelty to Animals (SPCA), 41, 81
Sohio, 20
Sports Illustrated, 61
Sprint, 108
St. Jude Hospital, 161
St. Lawrence Cement Company, 66
Starbucks Company, 8
Stiglitz, Joseph E., 4, 13
Stride Rite Corporation, 24, 168
Superfund Amendments and Reauthorization Act of 1986 (SARA Title III), 136
Susskind, Lawrence, 177 n.17, 178 n.1

Target Stores, 161
Texaco, 39
Thacker, Robert, 161
Thom McCann, 140
Thomas, Marlo, 161
Tommy Hilfiger, 2
Toyota, 3
Trabert, Richard, 95, 110
Tyco International, 6, 142, 169

United Parcel Service, 140
United Way, 37, 38, 39, 40, 87, 133, 145, 152

Urban League, 109
U.S. Home Corporation, 2
University of North Carolina, 164
University of Vancouver School of Community and Regional Planning, 74

Van Der Linde, Claas, 137

Wall Street Journal, 60
Wal-Mart, 2, 16
Walt Disney Company, 1, 15, 18, 57–66, 76, 95–96, 112
Washington Post, 58, 59, 64, 88, 159, 163
Watts, Philip, 171
Wegman, David, 62
Weill, Sanford, 169–70
Welch, Jack, 7, 20, 49, 50, 60–67, 95
Wells Fargo Company, 132
Wendy's, 40
Whitman, Christine, 60–63
Wilder, Douglas, 59
Wilkens, Roger, 58
Will, George, 59
Wolfe, Allan, 66
Woodward, C. Van, 58
World Bank, 21
World Economic Forum, 21
World Trade Organization (WTO), 3, 4, 5, 9, 21, 103, 115, 167
WorldCom, 6

Xerox, 145

Yankelovich, Daniel, 4, 24

Zebco Corporation, 20

Subject Index

AIDS, 43, 54
Attitude survey, 92

Book-of-the-Month Club strategy, 62–63
Boomer generation (self fulfillers), 23–28
Business case for corporate citizenship, ix, 40
Business ethics, 48

Cause marketing, 160–63
CEO role: in Company's charitable giving programs, 169–70; creating urgency, 102–5; setting global corporate citizen ship strategy, x, 167–68; social visionary, ix, 45, 48–51
CERES principles, 25
Citizen activism, 14–17
Collaboration and consultation strategy, 52–53
College binge drinking, 155–58
Combined Federal Campaign, 39
Command and Control relationships, 65–67
Communities, types of: common interest (functional), 81–82;

cyber, 81–82; employee, 80; fence-line, 80; impact, 80; spatial, 80
Community Advisory Panels, 25, 129–31
Community decision-making, 12–14
Community leadership, 82–86
Community planning, xi, 75
Community relations manager roles, 148–49
Community trust accounts, 72
Community vision, 45
Consult, Announce, Consult again, Decide, Implement, Compensate (CACDIC) strategy, 96
Corporate citizenship condition letter, 111–12, 165
Corporate philanthropy, 5, 7, 37–40, 55, 131, 134, 169; donor choice, 40; philanthropy matrix, 135
Corporate social responsibility, 25
Cyber activists, 36–37

Decide-Announce-Defend (DAD) strategy, 63–67
Donor incentive program, 142

Emotional intelligence, 94–95
Employee Involvement Program, 146
Employee voluntarism, 5: allowing released time for, 145; compensating employees for, 145–46; creating incentives for, 142; designing recognition and award programs for, 143; as a relationship building tactic, 140; as a skill development tactic, 140
Environment as part of community practice program, 136–37
Environmental stewardship, 25

Housatonic and Hudson River dispute, 7, 60–63, 65, 66, 67

General managers, role in corporate citizenship, 55
Global corporate citizenship strategy, x, 54
Globalization, 19–22
Government affairs strategy, 52

IBM: education strategy, 158–159; On Demand Community Strategy, 159–160
Internet, 22–23

Key Contact programs, 129
Kyoto Protocol, 24, 43

License to operate, 7, 53, 57, 84, 124
Lobbying, 6

Manager training program, 105–11
Mattapoisett cell tower incident, 29–31
Merck's move to Whitehouse Station, 69–73, 76

Needs assessment: community, 86; informal, 86–88
Neighbor of Choice concept, 124–25, 131
Nongovernmental organization contact program, 129

Opportunistic decision making, 43

Participatory planning, 74
Psychological contract, 126–28

Research and measurement, 146–47

Seeing is Believing program, 35–36
Self fulfillers, 65–66
Self fulfillment generation, 17–19
Site community strategy, 124–25, 128
Social connectors, 44
Social issues strategy, 163–65
Social vision, 45–53
Social visionary, 24, 45
Societal strategies, 167–71
Stakeholder defined, 91
Stakeholder relations, 79
Stakeholder relations plan, 99, 110, 121–22
The Standards of Excellence, 25–26
Stealing shamelessly with pride tactic, 111

Triple bottom line strategy, 36, 50, 165–67
Trust relationships, 93–94, 96–99, 128

United Way, 37–40

Walt Disney Co. and history theme park, 57–60, 64, 65, 66
White House Conference on Strategic Planning, xi

About the Author

EDMUND M. BURKE is founder and Director Emeritus of the Center for Corporate Citizenship at Boston College. The author of *Corporate Community Relations* (Quorum, 1999), he conducts seminars and training programs on corporate citizenship and consults to business leaders on issues of social responsibility and strategy.